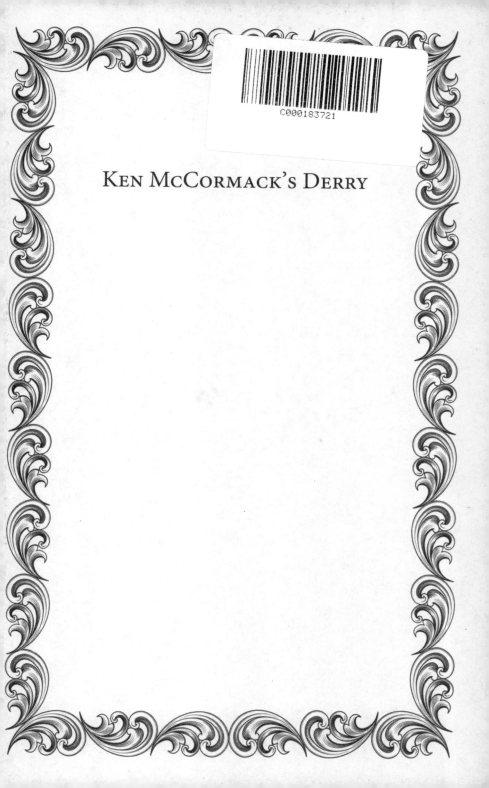

KEN McCORMACK'S DERRY

Ken McCormack's Derry

Ken McCormack

LONDUBH BOOKS

First published in 2010 by

Londubh Books

18 Casimir Avenue, Harold's Cross, Dublin 6w, Ireland

www.londubh.ie

1 3 5 4 2

Cover by bluett

Origination by Londubh Books

Printed in Ireland by ColourBooks, Baldoyle Industrial Estate, Dublin 13

ISBN: 978-1-907535-11-6

Dedicated to the memory of my dear parents, Phyllis and John

ACKNOWLEDGEMENTS

This book would never have seen the light of day but for the encouragement and assistance of Derry writer Sean McMahon. People have been asking for years why I have never published my stories and the answer is that I've kept putting them on the 'back burner' so to speak, making all sorts of excuses. Sean felt the time had come to remedy this and gave undivided attention to ensuring that I got down to collecting the material for this book. I am very grateful to him.

The stories themselves are the product of many decades of broadcasting and writing in various publications. I had the privilege of producing the first historical documentary on BBC Radio Foyle under the guidance of Ian Kennedy, and later Joe Mahon and Michael McGowan gave me a free hand in recounting the rich heritage of Derry and its surroundings. Stephen Price, former producer at Radio Foyle, was also very keen to see my stories in print and I would like to acknowledge his contribution. Thanks to those broadcasting colleagues who tramped the highways and byways with me – Susan McReynolds, Deirdre Donnelly, Colum Arbuckle, Michael Bradley, Mark Paterson and Frank Galligan.

I cannot thank the staff of Central Library in Derry enough for their tireless efforts, as is also the case for Martin McGinley, editor of the *Derry Journal*, William Allen, formerly of the *Belfast Telegraph*, and Ernie Falconer of *Waterside Voices*.

I am also most grateful to the local historian Annesley Malley; Frank McGurk, Carrigans; Richie Kelly, Killea; and Brendan Doherty of Prehen.

Last but not least my appreciation goes to my brother John

and my late brother Bernard for their constant support, and to all the people who passed stories to me along the way. I trust everyone will enjoy reading this book on Derry's intriguing folklore.

Contents

INTRODUCTION
DERRY, MY OLD CURIOSITY SHOP

Out of monuments, traditions, private records,
fragments of stories, passages of books and the like
we do save and recover somewhat from the deluge
of time...

Francis Bacon, 1623

Like the writer Kathleen Coyle I believe that Derry truly is a magical realm. Yet, strange as it sounds, sometimes you have to get away from a place really to make sense of it. My student and early working days saw to that, and sure enough when I was away from home I often found myself thinking about Derry and its past times. It was like looking in from the outside and it occurred to me then as it does now that we have an enormous wealth of folklore set in the most beautiful countryside you could ever wish to find. And somehow, here in the north-west we always seem to be at the forefront of making history – the era of Colum Cille, the Siege, the Famine, emigration from Derry Quay, the World Wars, Amelia Earhart's historic flight – the list is unending. Straight away I must say that for me history is not about dry dates. Rather it is about people, their activities and their emotions; the 'Bridge of Tears' and the 'Loneliness Stone' in Donegal are surely testimony to the sadness of the emigrants soon to depart from Derry Quay. I have this notion that people endow a place with their energies, not just their memories: something is stored where human beings have been. I remember when I was small and staying with my grandparents out in the country by the River Faughan (in Irish the 'sheltered place') I was told that there where places along the bank where spirits resided, akin to the nymphs of Ancient Greece and later my brother Bernard put the idea to great effect in his painting series 'Spirit of Place', using colour and form to depict the 'feel' of Celtic landscapes.

As I relate elsewhere in this book, when I was growing up I was fortunate to have parents who were born storytellers. Prompted by their tales, I wondered what it would be like to walk down Shipquay Street in bygone days or look up William Street and see St Eugene's Cathedral without its spire or a ship in full white sail embark from Derry Quay. And was there really a ghost in the Waterside workhouse? On and on it went. My imagination took flight, especially when my mother regaled me with stories of Half-Hanged McNaghten, the sinister 'Break-Neck' steps and how her grandfather had been employed in Watt's Distillery as a foreman and, lantern in hand, had to inspect the dark recesses of the endless vaults. In trips out into the country my father would point out haunted houses, big estates and old mills and buildings long since deserted, along the rivers and streams. Really, like Kathleen Coyle coming to Belt Cottage, it was as if it had all been waiting for my arrival. Even in those far-off times I made up my mind that one day I would record some of the great stories from my home place.

That said, storytellers must be careful with history, as it is very easy to glamorise events that may have been anything but pleasant. When soldiers returned to Holland from the Siege of Derry in 1689 and described what they had witnessed for artists, the result was a series of engravings that depicted Derry as a romantic place of towers and palaces in the manner of a magnificent medieval city – nothing like the overcrowded little Jacobean town it really was. Then, a century-and-a-half later, in 1840, William Bartlett, on his sketching tour of Ireland, set up his easel at the top of Bond's Hill in the Waterside and depicted Derry, with the old wooden bridge, as a quaint, rustic, almost fairytale town. True, the city was developing but how truthful was Bartlett's portrayal? Sometimes what people describe may not necessarily be the way things really are. Perhaps I should say there may be much more than what is depicted. Why, for example, did Lord Macaulay, the historian, not take a peep over Derry's walls down into the Bogside to give us some idea of the poverty and poor conditions there when he took that morning stroll in the late summer of 1849. With all these questions in mind I've attempted to put as much research as possible into my stories. It has meant much travel throughout the countryside to dwellings and locations where events took place – and many a night I've whiled away in haunted rooms. I've also spent hours in the dark corners of libraries and countless archives in an effort to uncover the true substance of what happened in Derry in bygone days.

A last word: I am often asked if I have a favourite tale or recollection about Derry or the wider north-west. I do and I think it's connected with memory. It's been said that some past experiences may be recalled through our sense of smell. Oliver Wendell Holmes, the great American author, wrote, 'Memories, imagination, old sentiments, and associations are more readily reached through the sense of smell than through any other channel.' I agree with this for I believe that somewhere deep in my limbic system lies a memory that seems at times to be conjured up in the manner of the bewitching aromas of an old curiosity shop. Before the era of supermarkets, Derry had some wonderful old-fashioned shops. I recall Rosborough's and the Home and Colonial Stores in Ferryquay Street, which in times past had the delightful name of Gracious Street. Shops like these had loose tea and sugar in chests, oranges in boxes, American apples, hams and bacon freshly sliced, and coffee milling machines that rumbled away noisily all day. So the aroma of freshly milled coffee wafted its way magically through the adjoining streets and seemed to draw the flavours of the other produce with it, seasoning the air in a most exotic almost mysterious way. Then there was McMichael's ship's chandler in Sackville Street: sail canvas, rope, wax, tarpaulins and varnish catching the nose in a dry, heady, almost acrid way. In the Waterside a little shop called Cheshire's had the most wonderful sweetish old-world aroma from the combination of confectionery, snuff and tobacco, while out in the country, in my aunt's Post Office Stores, which seemed to keep everything from a needle to an anchor, the aroma drifting in the air was the strangely hypnotic combination of foodstuffs, hams, sweets, metalware, paraffin and creosote.

I remember at school being intrigued by a story of H.G. Wells called 'The Magic Shop'. Wells evoked in that story the sense of everything that ever delights about the fantasy of magic. So it is with my own old curiosity shop – an Aladdin's cave of all the aromas that please the sensory system mixed together and contained therein. Of course such a shop never really existed but inside my head and my heart Derry has conjured it up for me.

Ken McCormack, October 2010

O Brave New World…

A Derry Family Secret

On a crisp December afternoon in 1975 a wisp of smoke curled its way into the cloudless blue sky from a back garden in Derry's Waterside. Soon what seemed a trivial fire became a substantial blaze as file after file of private papers and souvenirs was heaped upon the flames. It's reckoned that archival matter worth millions of pounds was burned that day, along with invaluable records and other material of immense local interest. Onlookers would not have realised it but what they were seeing was the result of a secret pact, the last bizarre chapter in the history of one of Derry's most noteworthy and eccentric families: the Loughreys of Clooney.

Derry has produced some remarkable personalities in its time and surely high on that list must be the Loughrey sisters, who had the pet names of Bird and Dill. They were known as the Miss Loughreys (sometimes the Misses Loughrey) and were famed the world over as breeders of Scottish deerhounds, large thick-coated dogs with very docile temperaments. The sisters were notably different: Bird, properly named Florence, was attractive, petite and feminine, while her younger sister Dill, or Hilda Mary, was haughty and domineering. Dill is remembered for her outlandish appearance; she wore a shirt and tie, a tweed jacket and skirt reaching down to her brogues. Perhaps the most remarkable item of her attire was her pork-pie hat. This was her trademark and it was rumoured that she bought a dozen of these bizarre hats at a time.

Bird and Dill had a brother, Edward, and they were the children of Joseph Loughrey, a successful solicitor with an office in Derry's Shipquay Street. Joseph's brother was the redoubtable and feisty Fr Edward Loughrey, the parish priest of Dungiven, who during a quarrel with Bishop McHugh in 1910 famously wrote: 'My Lord, I respectfully desire to inform you that I now go to Rome to lay my complaint in proper hands...' and whose story is told elsewhere in this book. It was, then, not in the Loughrey tradition to be shrinking violets and Bird and Dill maintained that tradition. They were frequently to be seen around Derry, perched regally in the rear of their Riley beach-wagon with brother Edward at the wheel. Edward was a retired brigadier who had served in the Sudan and had been something of a big-game hunter in his day. As a result he had brought back some very unusual souvenirs to Derry. Among them were a fearsome tiger-skin rug, two giant elephant-tusks and the stuffed heads of several wild animals. They had quite an effect on visitors to Rosslyn, the Loughrey home in Clooney.

Eccentric or not, the fame of Bird and Dill as deerhound breeders brought them adulation wherever they went. It was believed that no one could match Dill's handling of dogs in the show ring, while Bird's ability to spot a future champion was unequalled. Dill eventually became a renowned judge at Crufts. She was president of the London-based Deerhound Club for twenty-eight years and joint secretary/treasurer with Bird for twenty-three years. This made them acquainted with a select band of very wealthy people. When in London they used to stay at Brown's hotel in Mayfair, frequented by such luminaries as Theodore Roosevelt, Rudyard Kipling, Agatha Christie and even, on occasions, royalty. So high a profile had they that on the way to and from London they were welcomed personally by the captain of the Belfast ferry as VIPs and escorted to the best cabin.

The high point of their fame was the commissioning by the Kennel Club of Britain of a twenty-one-inch-high bronze of the great champion Prosthetic of Ross for their permanent exhibition. The actual subject of the sculpture was so valued that it was taken to America for safety during the Second World War. The question arises: if Bird and Dill Loughrey dominated the deerhound world from their Derry home throughout the twentieth century, what was the secret of their outstanding success? Herein lies a mystery that was eventually to lead to a bizarre pact between the sisters, which has left us with an unsolved riddle. The puzzle concerns the debate about the connection between Scottish deerhounds and Irish wolfhounds. At first glance the breeds seem not dissimilar. Yet Bird and Dill maintained that only the Scottish deerhound was pure-bred and that the Irish wolfhound was a crossbreed produced in the 1800s. To make matters worse, a relation of the Loughreys, Major H.D. Richardson, was partly responsible for the new wolfhound strain and this led to fierce internal family feuding.

In the end Bird and Dill Loughrey declared war on all Irish wolfhounds and their owners – even the mention of the name was enough to set Dill off at full tilt. Yet some wondered: did they protest too much? A typical instance occurred back in the 1960s when a young man brought his newly-purchased Irish wolfhound out to Rosslyn to seek advice about the breed. 'This is my new Irish wolfhound,' he said proudly to Dill Loughrey. 'It's nothing of the sort,' Dill replied curtly. 'That is a mongrel!'

Brian Doak, a local Scottish deerhound breeder, remembers his nervousness when he first went to Rosslyn. 'It was very daunting but I have to say they were most helpful,' Brian told me. 'They even showed me the spot where the great Loughrey champions were born.' What Brian saw was the famous Loughrey linen cupboard under the stairs in Rosslyn. It had almost the status of a shrine, for it was here that world-class deerhounds first saw the light of day.

All the Loughrey champions had names ending in 'ic': Ledric, Magic, Cleric, Osric and dozens more. But according to Brian, one of them, 'Tragic of Ross' (b. 1923), left its mark across the entire strain of Scottish Deerhounds everywhere. This name appears on practically every deerhound pedigree.

It is the gold standard. But are we any nearer to discovering how the Loughreys came to shape the world of deerhound breeding? What was the Loughrey secret? To understand we have to take a closer look at the sisters.

Firstly, both were very versatile: Dill had been a welder in an aeroplane factory during the First World War, while Bird had been a nurse treating soldiers with horrendous injuries. Bird later patented a cough balsam known as Miss Loughrey's Syrup of Carrageen Moss. It was said to ease away the winter blues and was popular throughout the 1940s and 1950s. Then we have to remember the assertive, sometimes flinty, Loughrey temperament. How the family came to prominence at Binnion in Donegal back in the 1800s is a story told elsewhere in this volume. It is the stuff that legends are made of and it left the sisters unshakable in anything they pursued; people in the world of dogs simply took their words as gospel. The sisters also gave their lives totally to their dogs. And a word of caution for ladies who aspire to breeding Scottish deerhounds. Apparently studies show that where women are concerned once they become addicted to the charm of the deerhound they want nothing more to do with men.

The Miss Loughreys were a case in point and some might argue that they even set the trend. Certainly one girl who came under their spell was the wealthy and beautiful heiress Nessy Linton, who had a string of young suitors. However, Nessy bought Dramatic of Ross from the Clooney kennels, won the trophy at Crufts (1932) and thereafter showed all her young men the door.

To get to the real heart of the mystery we have to move to the twilight of the Loughrey years in Derry. By the 1960s the sisters had considerably reduced their dog-breeding activities. Dill was still judging at Crufts, while Bird was writing for *Our Dogs* newspaper. Then one evening in the drawing room at Rosslyn they made an amazing decision – a pact that was to deny the world any details whatsoever of their champions, of their breeding expertise or of their family affairs.

The pact manifested itself in a similar clause in each of their wills. This stipulated that whichever of the sisters survived should arrange for every single piece of information relating to the Loughreys to be burned. News of the pact leaked out to the dog fraternity and sent shock waves through the Kennel and Deerhound Clubs. Plea after plea was made to Bird and Dill not to destroy their priceless records but to no avail. Then, as if to oblige, fate brought the curtain down on Derry's most eccentric pair. In 1969 Bird was crossing the road at a spot known locally as Dale's Corner to post an obituary to *Our Dogs* when she was struck by a vehicle and died instantly. Dill never recovered from Bird's death. A shadow of her former self, she tried to continue judging but eventually withdrew into her own lonely existence and died on 13 December 1975. In true Dill form before she departed she neatly boxed and labelled everything that was to be consigned to the flames – a fortune.

A dog breeder told me that the material burned in the garden at Rosslyn would be worth millions of pounds today. Also lost was the history of the family, including several epic tales of the Loughreys and their forebears. Yet the Clooney fire settled nothing. People soon began to ask why the Loughreys should want to burn their records in the first place. Strangely enough, it appears that one file had a famous name and a message written large on it: 'Tragic of Ross. Destroy!' This file contained the breeding details of the Loughrey's legendary Scottish deerhound. The minds of breeders went back to the deerhound-wolfhound argument and rightly or wrongly some pondered the unthinkable. Did Bird and Dill Loughrey secretly use an Irish wolfhound to refine their Scottish deerhound stock? If true, this information would have been the equivalent of an earthquake amongst the dog-breeding fraternity. As it turned out the answer went up in flames in December 1975 and to this day it remains the Loughrey secret.

A short time ago, while researching a history project in Dublin, I called on an old friend of Bird and Dill Loughrey. 'I remember them well,' my host told me. 'In fact, they left me a souvenir of Rosslyn!' I was led to a spacious drawing room and gasped, for there, taking up the whole length of a wall, was a giant elephant tusk. No amount of endeavour on my part could move it and I wondered if the indomitable sisters were smiling down on my efforts with their customary haughty self-assuredness!

From a Public Handbill

By Permission of his Worship the Mayor

The year of Our Lord 1790

In the Town Hall Londonderry this Evening

Saunders and Company

Equilibriums on the Slack Wire

(Without the assistance of a balance pole)

Mr Saunders will stand upon his head on a Quart Bottle on the Wire to Admiration, with many other surprising Equilibriums too tedious to insert.

Young Master Hunter will perform several amazing feats in Agility of Body.

Mr Saunders will then exhibit the Polanders inimitable Exhibition with a Peacock's Feather – truly singular and astonishing!

And to finish – several select Airs and Tunes on the much admired Musical Glasses.

Doors open at 7 o' clock

Tickets to be had at the Printer hereof

The Opera House: A Dream for Derry

Divas, Drama and Banter from the 'Gods'

'Derry 244…you're through to the box office…' This was the reply when you telephoned Derry's first and only Opera House in the early 1900s. These were times when the city was second to none in the world of the theatre. Yet all that remains today is a vacant site, a dreary little car park half-way up Carlisle Road. The Royal Opera House, later simply called the Opera House, was the realisation of the vision of a theatrical genius, James Warden, who brought his flair and money to the city when he realised how much Derry people hungered for entertainment.

The buzz around Derry in 1877 was palpable: at last the city was to get a proper theatre, something that would rival any in Ireland. There was excitement in the air as crowds gathered to see the elegant building take shape on Carlisle Road. It was to be known as the Royal Opera House, to give it an air of respectability, for there were many who viewed theatres as places of bawdy humour and low morals. Operas there would be – *Rigoletto, Il Trovatore, La Traviata* and more – but there would also be Shakespearean plays, comedy acts, music hall singers, concerts and even performances from amateur local groups. This then was the Derry Opera House – highbrow and lowbrow, whatever you wanted from arias to burlesque, vaudeville, dancing, drama and sing-alongs: a showbusiness kaleidoscope.

James F. Warden, the man who brought the Opera House to Derry, was originally from Hull. An actor since childhood, he knew just about everybody worth knowing in the world of the theatre: Henry Irving, Ellen Terry, Sarah Bernhardt and Frank Benson were just a few of the many great names he could call upon. After a sojourn in Belfast, Warden came to Derry in the late 1860s, where he performed in the Corporation Hall in the Diamond. Then gradually he began turning his energies to promotion and in a very short time was one of the country's leading impresarios.

An early success was the pairing of the so-called Derry giant Jimmy Allender with 'General Tom Thumb' – an act that saw the eight-foot-tall Allender pit his wits against Tom Thumb, the smallest man in the world. Audiences rolled in the aisles with laughter and it was this sort of show that had locals begging for a proper theatre with regular performances. Meanwhile, J.F. Warden and his wife, the aptly named Miss Jenny Bellairs, had taken a liking to Derry. The Wardens often performed together: Jenny Bellairs was a marvellous actress and an accomplished singer. Encouraged by the acclaim of the Derry audiences, the pair soon began to consider the possibility of building a dedicated theatre in the city. It was a risk. Apart from the Corporation Hall there was a theatre in London Street. Some argued that this was sufficient. Others would have pointed out that music hall entertainment lacked a proper venue in a period when vaudeville and burlesque were gaining a foothold elsewhere.

Knowing he could pull in the big names, Warden eventually decided to proceed with the venture. He invested his own money and obtained the services of the leading theatre architect of the day, Charles Phipps. He also hired theatre staff from Belfast, London, Edinburgh and Paris, to secure the best in stage and auditorium design. The location of Carlisle Road was chosen as there was land for development there and the rear of the building had access to the Glasgow boat terminal on the quay nearby. This meant that scenery and actors could depart quickly and easily to the next cross-channel venue via the rear of the Opera House.

Derry's brand-new Opera House opened on Friday 10 August 1877, a gala evening with the city fathers, special guests and many of those who had been involved with the construction. Warden himself took the leading role in the opening play and at the end stepped forward to a standing ovation. Yet, despite the adulation, not all of Derry approved. One local minister attacked the Opera House and labelled its clientèle 'thieves, drunkards and profligates...' Warden in reply said he would offer only the most wholesome entertainment and added, 'Our aim will be to instruct and elevate.' Most local people responded enthusiastically. Carriages and jaunting-cars from all parts, trams from Pennyburn and even trains from Buncrana in County Donegal brought crowds of people into the city, all bound for the new Carlisle Road theatre. Soon playbills were appearing in shop-windows and on street hoardings announcing the latest shows – *Black-Eyed Susan*, *Lady of Lyons* and *East Lynne*, to name but a few. Warden's idea was to stage something different each night of the week with the exception of Sunday. And his friends from the London stage did not disappoint him. Sir Edward Terry, Simms Reeve, Sir Frank Benson of 'Shylock' fame and the celebrated burlesque actress Jenny Willmore all trouped into Derry at Warden's behest. The stream of talent was unending.

In appearance the Opera House was an attractive two-storey red-brick building, with five tall arched windows on the first floor and a mansard roof (with sloped sides) containing a brick dormer with smaller circular-headed windows. Later the façade was faced with sandstone. At street level, entry was via three large doors, one of which took people up stone steps all the way to the top of the house. The lowest seating was referred to as the pit; the stalls were behind this area; then on the level above were the balcony and dress circle and finally under the roof was the gallery, commonly known as the 'gods'. In all, the Opera House could seat up to about fifteen hundred patrons. Descriptions of the inside suggest a breathtaking auditorium: walls and ceilings decorated with delightful motifs in ornamental plaster, flock wallpaper in green and gilt and plush red-velvet seats. On each side of the stage there were two sets of boxes draped in crimson. Lighting in the early days was by gaslight.

The climb up the stone steps to the 'gods' was a talking-point in Derry. When you reached the top your metal token was collected and rattled its way down a tube to the box office for the next customer. The seats here, the cheapest in the house, were no more than wooden benches, and it seems that the knees of the person behind you stuck into your back. People talked of feeling dizzy – and understandably so, for they were looking straight down into the auditorium.

It's no surprise to hear that the language in the 'gods' was robust and colourful, for the town's young men would gather at the top of the house to heckle the performers. Of course, people recognised that this banter was all part of the fun. A trip to the Opera House was a night to remember. After the initial surprise at the sumptuousness of the auditorium there was a hush as the orchestra struck up. Then the limelights would hiss into life and the curtain would rise to a deafening burst of applause as the first act took to the brilliantly-lit stage. At the interval, people were always fascinated by the safety curtain that slid down silently to reveal dozens of advertisements for local businesses.

Having made a success of the Opera House, Joseph Warden set his sights on Belfast once more. Here he purchased the Theatre Royal and then built the magnificent Grand Opera House, which opened in 1895 and still flourishes today. Ever energetic, this much-loved man continued to provide staggering promotions until his untimely death in 1898 at the age of sixty-two. Warden's departure from Derry brought new proprietors to the Carlisle Road venue, with a group called the Opera House Company Ltd. There was also a new manager in the shape of H.B. Phillips – a brilliant impresario who was to leave his mark on the Derry entertainment scene for decades to come. (His story also appears in this book.)

H.B. Phillips stayed with the Opera House for seven years, before leaving to run his own business. This left the door open for the genial Barney Armstrong, a suave, larger-than-life character, who smoked a cigar and greeted every customer like a long-lost friend. Barney continued with the vaudeville tradition and was also quick to spot new markets with travelling Irish theatre companies such as Charles Doran's and Anew McMaster's. But without a doubt Barney's trump card was the staging of the Ulster comedy with the controversial title, *The Pope in Killybuck*. There was considerable debate about this title and it was hastily changed before the opening night to the rather tame *The Auction in Killybuck*. Yet tickets were sold out for five weeks, leaving Barney smiling and the play with a record never to be broken in the Opera House's seventy years of existence.

Writer Sam Hughes, a connoisseur of the Opera House, recalled that pantomimes were also a great draw. Top English companies came to Derry from Belfast but Sam added, 'All the small-part players had Derry accents and when they weren't on stage they were busy selling tickets, shifting scenes or doing odd jobs about the place.' Another feature of the early 1900s was amateur dramatics and musicals, with shows like *The Desert Song* and the Gilbert and Sullivan operettas *The Mikado* and *The Pirates of Penzance* to the fore. Yet as the years moved on, despite regular visits from the D'Oyly Carte and Carl Rosa Opera companies, storm clouds gathered with the arrival of the movies. Sad to say, by the end of the 1920s audiences were so poor that the Opera House had to resort to showing films. Worse was to come, for in 1938 new owners decided that the great old theatre needed what I suppose would be called a makeover in modern parlance. Out went the beautiful ornate interior to be replaced with the trappings of the new art-deco style cinemas. Many Derry people were horrified and it almost seemed that the Opera House itself gave a sigh of despair. If such a thing happened then it was indeed a dying gasp, for oddly enough the building mysteriously burned to the ground after the Saturday film show of 9 March 1940.

It was, however, a great final curtain: flames leapt dramatically into the night sky, leaving a brilliant red and orange glow across Derry. Wartime blackout was in force and people recall that the reflections of the fire on the Foyle made it appear as if the river itself was burning. All that remained for curious sightseers on the way to Sunday morning church was a blackened shell and, bizarrely enough, a glass case advertising the coming week's attractions. Gone forever were the Italian operas, the burlesque and the vaudeville, the music-hall banter, the pantomimes and the local performers. If J.F. Warden had been alive to witness it, actor or not, I'm sure his tears would have been real ones.

Opera House Derry

Proprietor and Manager J. F. Warden

Mr Warden has much pleasure in announcing a short season of

Italian Opera

(For Five Nights only commencing Monday August 20, 1883.)

Il Trovatore, Rigoletto, Faust, Ernani, La Traviata

Principal Artistes:

Sopranos – Madame Evilina Servid, Theatre Royal, St Petersburg; Mlle Carolina Mosianj, Turin, Mlle Agnes de Laporte. La Scala Milan, Madame Portaluppi Palermo.

Tenors – Sig. Battista Baldini, Apollo Theatre, Rome, Sig. Paolo Bolli and Sig. Arturo Salvin, La Scala, Milan.

Baritones – Sig. Vittorio Bellati, St Petersburg, Sig. Stanislao Sorchi, Naples.

Bassos – Sig. Paolo de Benghardi, Grand Opera House, Paris, Sig. Natale Moro, Turin.

Full orchestra and chorus of 50 performers from Italian and Paris Opera Houses

Conductor--Signor A De Gabrielle, Theatre Royal, Naples.

Admission: Boxes 36s and 24s, Balcony 6s, Upper Circle 3s, Pit 2s and Gallery 1s.

Doors open at 7 o' clock; Commence at 7.30.
Tel: Derry 244

THE FOLLY OF ANDREW WATT

*How Derry's Great Whiskey Empire
Came Tumbling Down*

The Watts of Thornhill, near Derry, owned one of the world's great distilleries. Located at Abbey Street in Derry's Bogside, it produced famous brands such as the 'Tyrconnell' and 'Inishowen' and made a fortune for the family. Then one bleak day in Derry, after workers clashed with management, the Watts responded by closing the whole process forever. It sent shock waves through the entire whiskey industry and left a legacy of poverty in Derry that was to last for decades to come. But was it a moment of madness, or was there something more sinister to it all?

Picture this: a gleaming yellow Rolls Royce is slowly making its way through the Bogside in the gloom of a cold foggy morning in 1921. The air is tense and there are huddles of men everywhere. Unbelievably, the workers of Watt's Distillery are on strike. The eight-acre site, normally humming with activity round the clock, is as silent as the grave. In the approaching vehicle is sixty-eight-year-old Andrew Alexander Watt and he's intent on a showdown. As the limousine draws up at the Abbey Street entrance to the distillery on this awful morning a crowd of workers moves forward and blocks the gates. Defiant shouts and cheers suddenly echo through the narrow streets. Then, just as quickly, there's a hush as Andrew Watt steps from his Rolls. His grim countenance says it all – he is ready for a fight.

The Watt family reputation was built on generations of hard graft. The Watts were stubborn and flinty and never flinched from a dispute. Andrew Watt maintained the tradition well. He was a small dapper man, sharp-featured and with a bristling moustache. A.A., as he was popularly known, dressed impeccably and carried himself with an almost military bearing – in all he presented a formidable picture. Even before the strike was called, old hands about the Bogside had cautioned, 'Don't argue with the Watts. They'll never back down.' Yet there was total frustration amongst the workers, who insisted they couldn't live on the wages they were getting. Watt had dismissed their pleas out of hand, declaring that there was no money in the whiskey trade due to a decline in sales.

So on this memorable day it was mutiny. Suddenly, Andrew Watt was prevented from entering his own distillery and, worse still, he was all but submerged in a crowd of enraged workers. What happened next must rate high in the annals of Derry's dark days. Andrew Watt asked to be helped up on to one of his own whiskey barrels and from there he addressed the crowd with the menacing words: 'Well, men, I shall put it to you like this ... what is it to be? Will you open the gates?'

The workers retorted angrily: 'The gates stay shut!'

'Very well!' exclaimed Watt bluntly. 'Shut they are and shut they shall remain!'

In this bleak instant Watt's whiskey enterprise disappeared from Derry forever. Over three hundred jobs were lost, including the talents of some of Ireland's finest whiskey blenders. Also left jobless were coopers, carpenters and a host of other tradespeople and office staff, many of whose parents and grandparents had worked for Watts for generations. As for A.A. Watt, he, too, left the city, never to return. In doing so he turned his back on what would be a multi-million pound business in today's world.

Looking back the outcome can be viewed as nothing less than a total disaster. The loss was staggering. The Watts had two sites in Derry, one at Abbey Street and the other at Spencer Road in Waterside (where the health centre is now located). The city-side distillery made grain whiskey, while pot-still whiskey (single malt) was produced at the Waterside premises. Estimates on the total output vary but it seems that the two plants between them produced up to two million gallons of whiskey in 1900. Output rose to six million gallons when other distilleries were brought on board. Incidentally, much of Watt's bottling and administration was done at 33 Shipquay Street, Derry. The site stretched back almost a hundred yards to the city walls. There were also production facilities in Belfast.

At the time the Watts' operation in Derry was probably the biggest of its kind in the world. An idea of the scale comes from the fact that the two multi-storey granaries at Abbey Street were the size of football pitches; the mixing vessels were twenty feet deep and it took a 50,000 gallon tank to feed the Coffey stills. These stills were the talk of the country for they were as tall as skyscrapers and dwarfed St Eugene's Cathedral until it got its spire. But towering above everything were the two giant chimneys, one-hundred-and-sixty and one-hundred-and-thirty feet high. Apparently they could be seen for miles and were a landmark for ships coming into Derry in the days of sail.

Distilleries in those days were dark, cavernous places. You can imagine the incessant noise from the grinding mills, the steam engines and the workshops. Conditions were often deplorable. Everyone knew that you risked getting lost or injured, or even drowned, in a distillery. No wonder then that the workers were begging for higher wages. Yet one thing can be said of the Watts: they were well ahead of their time in their use of innovations and technology. It was this fact that left competitors trailing in their wake. Anyone who ran foul of them could expect no quarter – litigation and buy-outs were the order of the day if you squared up to this tenacious Derry outfit. And out of this came the celebrated spirits, which made Watts a worldwide name. A major reason for their success is that in the beginning they were fortunate to get the services of the brilliant Aeneas Coffey, whose patent still invention revolutionised the whiskey trade. Coffey came to Derry in 1833 and the Watts never looked back.

The Watt family came to the city in 1762 from Ramelton in County Donegal. Firstly, they established a business in wines, spirits and general merchandise in Bishop Street. Then in the early 1800s they moved into whiskey distilling at Abbey Street under the direction of David Watt. A.A., who was David's nephew, took over the reins in the 1870s and from this date the company expanded across the globe. A.A. had been educated at Foyle College but also had a private tutor. He was made High Sheriff for County Londonderry in 1886 and loved hunting and shooting in his spare time. Watt was sharp-witted and uncompromising. Most of all he had a vision – he wanted to own one of the biggest distilleries in the world and it appears he also wanted to dominate the Scottish whisky industry. This latter ambition was a bridge too far.

Andrew Watt's first major attempt at empire-building came in 1902 when he amalgamated with two Belfast distilleries to form the United Distilleries Company. Next he turned his eyes towards Scotland, where the Distillers Company reigned. After a bitter dispute the two groups agreed to divide the spoils and to seal the bargain they each took shares in the other's company. Shortly afterwards Watt ran foul of the Scottish group again when he opened a finance company in a bid to control the smaller distilleries in Scotland. This proved his undoing, as changes in the spirit laws and Prohibition in America in 1919 began to limit his cashflow. Soon, Andrew Watt found himself in the humiliating position of having to ask his Scottish rivals to take over his company. Some people maintain that a fire at Abbey Street in 1915 was the beginning of the end for the Watts. The vats had to be opened and it seems whiskey flowed along the gutters, much to the delight of the locals, it must be said, for they were able to collect bucketfuls of the precious spirit. But the real damage was done by A.A. Watt's expansionist tendencies. Quite simply he bit off more than he could chew and left his whole operation vulnerable to a take-over.

There may have been other unseen factors at work in the

shock closure of the Derry distilleries. By the beginning of the 1920s the city and surrounding countryside was in a state of great tension due to the Irish Troubles. Did Andrew Watt wonder if the proposed partition of Ireland would affect his business and his estate? Was he looking for a way out? Or was he just exhausted by all the tribulations of the whiskey industry? Whatever the case he left Derry and spent his retirement at Easton Hall in Lincolnshire. It was one of the great stately homes of England, close to Margaret Thatcher's birthplace at Grantham. Here the former whiskey magnate remained until his death in 1928, at the age of seventy-five.

What occupied him in his twilight years? Perhaps he remembered the great days in 1876 when his chestnut colt, 'Tyrconnell', won the National Produce Stakes in Dublin at 100 to 1. He named a single malt spirit after the horse and thus one of the world's finest whiskeys, the 'Tyrconnell', was born. Or, maybe he recalled evenings in his famous London club Boodle's – the domain of the aristocracy, prime ministers, philosophers and writers such as Ian Fleming. There may even have been a smile on his face at the thought of the day he and his wife Violet met Queen Victoria at court. Did he present her with a bottle of the famous Derry spirit, I wonder? Sadly, back here, in Derry, no such luxury. The legacy of the closure of Watt's was unemployment and poverty in the dark days of the 1920s. It was to be 1925 before the old distilleries at Abbey Street and Waterside were finally dismantled. Strangely enough, there were still thousands of gallons of spirits in Watt's vats and this whiskey continued to be sold through a trading company called Iriscots until 1972.

The last vestige of Watt's empire still standing in the city is the old warehouse on Distillery Brae, Waterside. Many quality whiskies were stored here. It was said that the original Watt's single malt whiskey made in Derry outdid all its Scottish counterparts. And astonishingly the spirit now lives on. The famous 'Tyrconnell' was reincarnated in 1988 by the Cooley Distillery in Dundalk, County Louth. Produced mainly for the American market, it is already a major prizewinner in the league of great whiskeys. Connoisseurs describe it as golden in colour, with a supreme aroma and a mildly sweet taste of oranges, lemon and spice. It brings to mind the old joke that the aroma around Watt's Distillery in the city in past times was so potent that passers by always lingered a while to get the full advantage of the famous 'Derry Air'.

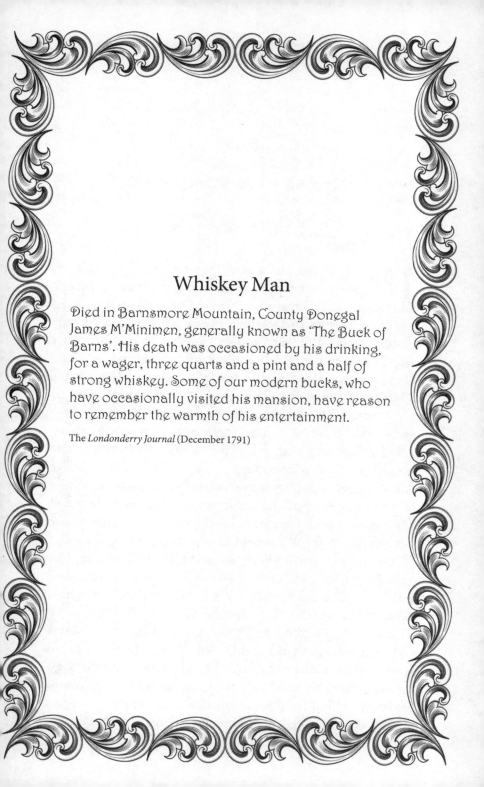

Whiskey Man

Died in Barnsmore Mountain, County Donegal
James M'Minimen, generally known as 'The Buck of
Barns'. His death was occasioned by his drinking,
for a wager, three quarts and a pint and a half of
strong whiskey. Some of our modern bucks, who
have occasionally visited his mansion, have reason
to remember the warmth of his entertainment.

The *Londonderry Journal* (December 1791)

CORDNER'S FLYING MACHINE

'A Lonely Impulse of Delight'

Though it is hard to believe, the first aeroplane to take to the skies in this part of the world was made of bicycle parts. This flimsy affair was the brainchild of adopted Derryman, Joseph Cordner, who assembled the plane secretly in 1908 in a bid to make the first flight in Ireland. Cordner truly was a magnificent man in his flying machine.

When Joseph Cordner and his twin brother Edward came to Derry in 1908 you'd never have guessed that pioneering air flights were on their minds. Their first move was to set up a bicycle repair business in John Street on the River Foyle's west bank. This they ran with great success and soon the brothers were familiar figures, often seen cycling across Carlisle Bridge from their home at King Street in the Waterside. Yet all the while they'd been gathering the parts to make an aeroplane and these bits and pieces were stored at the John Street shop, where most people thought they were merely repairing bicycles. Of the two Cordner brothers, Edward (Ed) kept a rather low profile but you couldn't miss Joe, as he was popularly called. He had a striking appearance: a small, dapper man, with a neat moustache, he wore a flat cap, jacket and knickerbockers.

By all accounts the two brothers, then aged thirty-three, were brilliant repairmen and could turn their hands to anything. This was no surprise for, as the sons of Armagh farming folk, they were used to doing all sorts of jobs and both had been in the cycle business for many years in Lurgan. Joe had also acquired a knowledge of motorcycle engines

– a rarity here in those times. In fact, Derry had seen its first automobile just eight years earlier, in 1900. One might ask what brought the Cordners all the way to Derry. At a guess it was a case of 'the hungry eye sees far': to be precise, from Lurgan the beaches of Lisfannon and Magilligan would have seemed highly attractive for a fledgling air pioneer, not just for the conditions but also for the privacy. To understand why they wanted to do things in secret it must be remembered that Ireland had not even seen an aeroplane by 1908. In fact, it was only five years earlier that the Wright brothers, Orville and Wilbur, had staged the first powered flight in history at Kitty Hawk Beach, North Carolina. They achieved a distance of only thirty-nine metres but their flight was to change the world for ever.

Suddenly there was a craze amongst engineers and mechanics to build their own planes. The competition was massive and you certainly didn't want your competitors to know what you were doing. All the while, the question on everyone's mind was: who would make the first flight outside America. Then news came to Joe Cordner in Derry that Samuel Cody, an American who had become a British citizen, had made a powered flight at Farnborough in England in October 1908: a thousand feet in twenty-nine seconds. If Cordner needed a spur, this was it. He wanted the honour of making the first flight in Ireland so straight away he got down to serious work. Joe Cordner was a genius when it came to inventions and now he brought all the pieces of his prototype plane together. Part of the frame consisted of metal tubing from bicycles; the four wheels also came from bicycles, the wings were made of canvas, each fifteen feet in width, and the whole assembly was to be fastened together with dozens of yards of piano wire.

Then came the vital part, the engine, which was really a motorcycle engine or at least a modified version of one. It was known as the 'JAP' engine, short for J.A. Prestwich Industries. This was a very versatile single-cylinder four-stroke engine that airmen were already experimenting with. Joe was familiar with the JAP and knew he could thoroughly depend on it. With powered flight now achieved in England, the newspapers were predicting that Ireland's aspiring aviators would be in the air in 1909. So if Joe Cordner wanted to be first he had only the closing months of 1908 at his disposal. Joe's main rival was none other than the great Harry Ferguson of tractor fame. Harry, based in County Down, and reckoned to be one of the most inventive minds in the country, was hot on Joe's heels.

But how could you keep a plane secret in the Derry of 1908? For Joe Cordner the answer was simple: he put all the parts in wooden boxes and labelled them 'Machine Parts'. Then from John Street the boxes were taken by horse and cart to the Lough Swilly Railway Station at the bottom of Strand Road (roughly where Sainsbury's is today). At this stage we have to distinguish between myth and reality. Firstly, the story goes that Joe and his party set out for Fahan on a morning in the last week of October 1908. With Joe were his brother Ed, an engineer friend called Pratt and Ernest G. Harries, a well-known Derry photographer, based in Bishop Street. It's also likely that Joseph Cordner's eldest son, Joe, was present.

I'm sure there would have been gasps had the people of Derry, Bridgend, Tooban Junction or Fahan known that the bits and pieces of a flying machine were speeding along the track on the Buncrana train. Joe's destination was Fahan Station, where the party alighted and transported the boxes to the White Strand at Lisfannon, just outside Buncrana. They went unnoticed – it was nearly winter and a hundred years ago these parts were much more deserted than they are today. The famous words of Orville Wright when he arrived at Kitty Hawk beach must have been echoing in Joe's head as he looked at the beach: 'We came down here for wind and sand and boy do we have them!' It was the same at Lisfannon's White Strand – flat sand and a stiff breeze that would give the plane all the necessary lift.

You might well believe that Joe Cordner's plane was a

very rickety affair. The makeshift wings spanned thirty feet and apart from the four wheels the rest was wire and metal tubing. In truth the only solid part was the JAP engine. The whole arrangement was as light as a feather and, as someone remarked at the time, one good gust would have blown it far out to sea. As we shall see those were ominous words. The pilot was perched in the middle of this extraordinary contraption and completely unprotected. At the time Joe was not a pilot. One might wonder who the pilot was back then. Anyway, Pratt elected to have the first go and sure enough when the plane was faced into the wind and the engine got up to speed it lifted several feet off the beach. All hands followed in hot pursuit, with cries of jubilation. But the elation was short-lived. A sudden blast of wind swept the plane sideways and the onlookers watched with horror as it first up-ended and then nose-dived into the sand. The pilot scrambled from the wreckage bruised and cut by the piano wire – indeed it proved to be his last adventure in the air. Yet Joseph Cordner's plane had flown and tradition holds that the first flight in Ireland took place in Lisfannon that October day in 1908.

But was it true? Did it happen this way? The only evidence for Joe Cordner's historic flight comes from Harry Swan, the Buncrana historian. According to Swan, Joseph Cordner made the first powered flight in Ireland in Lisfannon in 1908. Swan himself was not there to see it but he was present years later when Cordner himself described the flight. True as this may be, you find others saying that Joe really never got off the ground until 1909 or 1910.

In the meantime, Harry Ferguson, with a dedicated team of workers, began to overtake Joe Cordner. Harry achieved the first officially-recognised flight in Ireland at Hillsborough in County Down in 1909. It's believed that both Cordner and Ferguson built their early planes to specifications that appeared in a mechanics magazine. The two aviators combined forces at Magilligan in 1910, when Harry Ferguson decided that the long County Derry beach offered the best conditions for flying in the north of Ireland. As for Joe himself, it's certain that he was flying in the north-west in 1912, for this fact is mentioned in a publication of the time. By now he had abandoned the JAP engine and settled for a French model instead. Eventually, Joe and Ed Cordner moved house from King Street to nearby Pine Street, where there was plenty of space at the back for working at their machines.

At this time there was an open space in the Waterside called Bond's Field and for a while Joe used this nearby venue for short experimental flights. It proved to be very restrictive and soon he moved further down the Clooney Road to the flat land at Campsie. It was in Campsie that Joseph Cordner was almost overtaken by disaster. It seems his son Joe was steadying the plane after his father had started the engine and was preparing to climb on board. But the engine developed so much power that the efforts of father and son were not enough to restrain it. Eventually, they were forced to let go, with the result that the plane went off by itself. The pair watched with alarm as it made speed and momentarily took to the air before crash-landing, no doubt greatly relieved to have escaped injury. Incidentally, just to illustrate how dangerous it was, Samuel Cody's plane broke up while he was flying in England in 1913 and he was killed, along with his passenger.

With the arrival of the First World War, Joe Cordner joined the Royal Flying Corps and in 1916, at just over the age of forty, he became an officially-trained pilot. Based at Hendon, near London, he used his now considerable skills to teach young aviators. After the war we find Joe back in the north-west, running sightseeing flights in Portrush in the summer season of 1919 in an old First World War plane. This aircraft began to develop problems and was eventually dispensed with. But with the Derry cycle business still thriving Joe was able to turn his mind to more inventions. He had already worked on preliminary designs for air brakes and wing flaps but by now helicopters had become his passion. He drew up plans for helicopter flight and demonstrated that his ideas could work by means of a toy model.

Somewhere along the way Joe Cordner linked up with another great Derry character, Lester Jackson. Among other things, Lester set about fabricating the flaps for Joe's planes. He was brilliant when it came to anything mechanical and was equally at home working with wood, especially in finishing polished surfaces. It would be fair to say that although they didn't get credit for it, many of the designs that Cordner and Jackson worked on are used in one way or another on today's aeroplanes. They were two geniuses ahead of their time.

In 1937, at the age of sixty-two, Joe Cordner felt it was time to call it a day and moved from Derry to Belfast. However he never lost his passion for inventing and for many years continued with his helicopter ideas. Joseph Cordner, Derry's great aviation pioneer, passed away in 1963 at the grand old age of eighty-eight.

As an aside, I may mention that I had the opportunity to interview Lester Jackson in my early broadcasting days. He was a lively, very intense man, with quite penetrating eyes – not the sort that would suffer fools gladly, I thought. There wasn't much talk of Joe Cordner as Lester led me into a darkened room, where to my horror I witnessed what I thought were eight coffins lined against the walls. About a minute later I nearly jumped out of my skin as eight clocks chimed simultaneously and loudly. What I had taken for coffins were really grandfather clocks, Lester's latest craze and finished quite beautifully, I might say. Obviously pleased with the shock he'd given me, Lester leaned over towards me with eyes bulging and quipped, 'I like to be on time, don't you know!' We both had a good laugh afterwards and I've since thought there must have been some exciting days when Joe Cordner and Lester Jackson teamed up to work on their amazing flying machines.

Balloon Ascent

On Saturday evening last the inhabitants of Derry
were much amused to view the novel spectacle of
the ascent of a balloon upon Joseph Montgolfier's
primitive principle of the rarification of the air
inside by heat. The balloon was six feet in height,
presenting a magnificent appearance in mid-air.
It wafted down the river and disappeared about
Moville.

The *Londonderry Journal* (1837)

THE GREAT H.B. PHILLIPS

When World Stars Came Trouping to Derry

Back in the early 1900s, long before the arrival of television, some of the most celebrated musicians in the world – stars in their own right – loved to perform in Derry. This attraction to the city came as a result of their affection for one man, a local man with extraordinary charm and persuasive powers, not to mention musical talent: the remarkable H.B. Phillips. Henry Bettesworth Phillips, H.B. to his friends, holds a legendary place in the league of great impresarios. He helped to put Derry on the map; he established Ireland's greatest music shop in Derry and he still found time to manage the famous Carl Rosa Opera Company.

To begin with let me take you back to the Saturday morning of 8 February 1936, when people on Derry's Culmore Road gasped at an amazing sight. A tall, elegant black man was jogging in a leisurely manner along the thoroughfare behind a sedate old-fashioned Austin car. It was none other than the great American bass-baritone Paul Robeson, who was visiting the city at the behest of a much-revered local man and had expressed the wish to do some light exercise. Getting Robeson to come to Derry was a master stroke for music promoter H.B. Phillips. Robeson was unsurpassed as a singer, universally acclaimed as an actor and as if this wasn't enough he was outstanding in top-flight football, baseball, basketball and athletics. Yet, unbelievably, here he was in Derry. He had completed the film *Sanders of the River* in Hollywood in 1935 and went on to make the classic movie *Showboat* the same year.

But I really should begin the Phillipses' story with a curious incident that occurred just over a decade later, in 1947. On Thursday evening, 16 May, something happened on Shipquay Street that had all Derry talking: the massive plate-glass window of H.B. Phillips's music shop was shattered into a thousand pieces. To be truthful people didn't know whether to laugh or cry, for on the one hand the episode was comical, while on the other it brought an end to one of Derry's great landmarks. The Phillipses' window, occupying the full frontage of their shop, Beethoven House, was reputed to be the largest in Europe. When the dust had settled, so to speak, the *Derry Journal* reported that two sailors a little the worse for drink were larking about in front of the Phillips's premises. One took at race at his companion and both went through the shop window, with devastating consequences. As it so happened, at the time, the curtain was slowly coming down on the man who installed that famous window and made the shop something of a local institution. H.B. Phillips, the renowned Derry impresario, would be dead just three years later, at the age of eighty-two.

I mention the big window and the shop for it was typical of Phillips. Somehow he managed to do things with style, yet modestly and without show. Local people took greatly to H.B. and the stars adopted him as one of their own. Among his acquaintances were celebrities such as Enrico Caruso, Count John McCormack, Ellen Terry, Dame Nellie Melba, Dame Clara Butt, Sir Thomas Beecham, Paul Robeson, Richard Tauber and the magnificent soprano, Dame Joan Hammond.

H.B. Phillips was born in County Kilkenny in 1866 and came to Derry at the age of ten as a chorister in St Columb's Cathedral. He was schooled at Foyle College and became an apprentice in a local music establishment before training with a leading London piano company. This thorough grounding in music soon paid dividends, for by the age of twenty-four he had opened his own music business and promoted the first major concert ever to take place in Derry's Guildhall.

H.B.'s first premises were in Union Place in Derry. By 1896 he had taken over the management of Derry Opera House and soon he was able to set himself up as a countrywide booking agent for musical events. Then in 1901 he opened Beethoven House at 30 Shipquay Street and later used the same name for his Belfast undertaking. The Derry shop at Shipquay Street surpassed all others in the country. Pianos were a Phillips speciality. A catalogue shows you could buy a top-class piano for £22 in 1914. You could also purchase the latest recordings and almost any musical instrument or musical score was available at Beethoven House. All manner of instruments were repaired there and it served as a booking office for musical shows. No surprise then that people flocked to the Phillipses' shop for almost eighty years. It was bright and welcoming and had a very special atmosphere. There was always the sound of music and you could browse to your heart's content, meet your friends and even hear the latest goings-on about town.

H.B. married Annette Prior in 1904. People may recall Prior's magnificent old-world chemist shop in Derry's Ferryquay Street. Nettie, as she was known, was the daughter of the family and later became an acclaimed concert pianist. Their daughter Ailne (b. 1905) was the famous 'Babs' of the Royal Ballet (Sadler's Wells). Babs was an outstanding ballerina and inseparable friend of the great Dame Ninette de Valois. She also danced for the Carl Rosa Opera Company, which H.B. Phillips first managed and later acquired, in the early 1900s. His idea was to bring classical music to everyone but in the beginning the Carl Rosa all but drained H.B.'s personal finances. He later recalled how on one evening the box office takings were only £2 at a time when the weekly outlay was £800. Yet, typically of the man, he stayed with it and eventually made the company an outstanding success.

All the while H.B. was forging great contacts in the world of music; the outstanding conductors, Sir Thomas Beecham, Sir Henry Wood and Hans Richter, became his personal friends and he could call on all the leading performers of the day.

Eventually he shifted his home to London but continued to run concerts in Derry's Guildhall and in Belfast's Ulster Hall. He reserved some of the greatest moments for Derry. Among these were the performances of Count John McCormack, the world famous tenor, Fritz Kreisler, probably the outstanding violinist of the time, and the magnificent Paul Robeson.

McCormack came to Derry three times for H. B. Phillips. As you might guess there was not a dry eye in the house when he sang his Irish ballads in the Guildhall. In 1932 he said to H.B., 'Do you know it's twenty-three years since my last visit here. That makes me feel old but I hope it won't be my last trip to Derry.' Kreisler, he who had been in his time a medical student, a soldier in the trenches, a brilliant chess player, a composer and world-class violinist, didn't like the Derry weather. So in order to settle his nerves before taking to the Guildhall stage he went to see the latest Mae West film, *Going to Town,* at the Palace Cinema, which was just beside the Phillipses' shop in Shipquay Street. Kreisler preferred to be accompanied by a Steinway grand piano but Phillips had no such instrument in stock at the time. To everyone's relief it turned out that Colhouns, a well-known local family, had a Steinway and would gladly make it available if it could be tuned to Kreisler's satisfaction. As a result a special tuning fork was despatched post-haste to Derry from the Steinway headquarters in London and the concert went ahead with many encores.

As for Paul Robeson, apart from his jogging, he expressed delight about being in Derry and wanted to see the scenery around the city. It had a magical effect for his concert has been rated one of the most memorable events ever to occur here. The Guildhall was so packed that the stage was used for additional seating. Robeson and his pianist were all but submerged as favourites such as 'Swing Low, Sweet Chariot', 'Joe Hill' and 'Ol' Man River' mesmerised the massive audience. Successful or not, an idea of just how difficult it was for H.B. Phillips to stage such an event can be seen in the balance sheet for the Robeson concert. This shows that H.B. barely made £13, a fraction of the overall takings, which mainly went to the singer and his London agent.

Phillips was clearly not making a fortune and it was only his love of music and his desire to bring its joys to a wider public that kept him going. He had, of course, the support of a loving family but with the Carl Rosa making constant demands he passed control of Beethoven House in Derry to his younger brothers, George and Arthur. By 1948 he was able to report that business was flourishing – the Derry shop was in good hands and the Carl Rosa was so big it took seven trucks to carry the company's twenty tons of scenery. Even at the age of eighty, H.B. was making plans to bring music into cinemas. People remember him as a small, astute, charming man – always enthusiastic and encouraging, and above all persuasive. These attributes were with him all the way until his death in 1950.

In later times the ownership of Beethoven House passed down to Ken and Eric Phillips (sons of Arthur) but by 1980, with no one in the family able to take over, it was decided to sell the business. Oddly enough, when a forgotten store at the back of the shop was being cleared out, a grand piano came to light. People wondered if it had accompanied some of the great stars of earlier days. Also uncovered was an Edison Phonograph, a souvenir from H.B.'s first days in 1901. It was in mint condition and in perfect working order.

One further memento encapsulates the achievements of H.B. Phillips as an impresario – the autograph album, as it is known in the family. H.B. asked all his performers to sign the little leather-bound book. You find inside a message from Caruso and a sketch of himself, a quip from John McCormack, warm words form Paul Robeson and Joan Hammond – and on it goes. It is a treasure trove of signatures of the most renowned singers and musicians of bygone times. Also in the album two unique and famous signatures stand out, those of Amelia Earhart (May 1932) and General Balbo (July 1933).

Both flew into Derry; Amelia landed in a field in Ballyarnett, while Balbo's flying boat touched down on the River Foyle. In a strange way fate seemed to have guided them here but it's a measure of the fame of Beethoven House that they both came to visit Derry's great music shop.

POSTSCRIPT

Back for a moment to that notorious incident of the smashing of the Shipquay Street window into smithereens in 1947. The comical side of the incident was not lost on Derry folk or on H.B. Phillips for, strange to say, the solicitor who represented H.B. when he eventually made a claim for damages for the smashed window was none other than a Mr Glass!

A plaque at the beautiful little St Paul's Church, the actors' church, in London's Covent Garden, commemorates H.B. Phillips and his wife Annette. They are in good company, for remembered alongside this wonderful Derry couple are artists such as Ellen Terry, Gracie Fields, Vivien Leigh, Noel Coward and Charlie Chaplin. At the site of the Shipquay Street shop a Blue Plaque now honours the memory of Henry Bettesworth Phillips – the Great H.B.

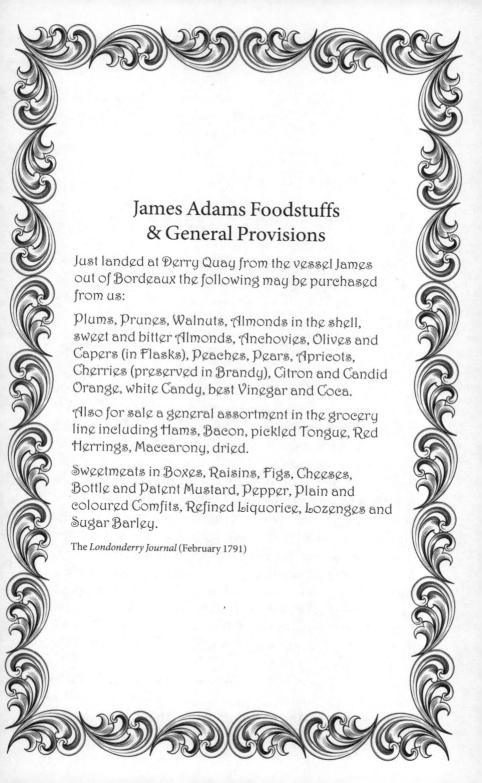

James Adams Foodstuffs
& General Provisions

Just landed at Derry Quay from the vessel James out of Bordeaux the following may be purchased from us:

Plums, Prunes, Walnuts, Almonds in the shell, sweet and bitter Almonds, Anchovies, Olives and Capers (in Flasks), Peaches, Pears, Apricots, Cherries (preserved in Brandy), Citron and Candid Orange, white Candy, best Vinegar and Coca.

Also for sale a general assortment in the grocery line including Hams, Bacon, pickled Tongue, Red Herrings, Maccarony, dried.

Sweetmeats in Boxes, Raisins, Figs, Cheeses, Bottle and Patent Mustard, Pepper, Plain and coloured Comfits, Refined Liquorice, Lozenges and Sugar Barley.

The *Londonderry Journal* (February 1791)

Derry: The Magical Realm

The City through a Writer's Eyes

If there is one writer who truly evokes Derry in past times for me it is Kathleen Coyle. When I was young my parents and grandparents used to regale me with stories about Derry in bygone days. And so I used to wonder what it was like to wander through our streets: to see tall ships on Derry Quay or walk down Shipquay Street (or Silver Street as was) or Gracious Street, now Ferryquay Street, or view the old-fashioned shops in the Diamond or the Strand or smell freshly ground coffee in stores bulging with foodstuffs. Although it has all gone – is history now – in a way it will be always be with me. In a similar fashion it seems to me that Kathleen Coyle carried Derry memories with her on her travels.

Kathleen Coyle, who died in 1952, aged sixty-six, is one of the great unsung writers of the north-west. Somehow she achieved more recognition internationally than locally and it's no surprise to hear that she could list James Joyce and Rebecca West among her admirers. Her idea was that history is never left behind but journeys with us in spirit, providing the opportunity to understand ourselves and the world we live in. This she highlights beautifully in her book, *The Magical Realm*, recalling a wonderful Derry childhood. For me it is the only writing that truly reveals what it was like to live in Derry at the beginning of the last century.

The Magical Realm was written in the early 1940s in America as Kathleen's health was beginning to fail. I feel it is easily her best work. In it she conveys to us the awe and wonder of the world seen through the eyes of a child. At the same time she does not overlook the darker side: women imprisoned in frustrating relationships, battling tirelessly to change their men. Her own father, John Coyle, was a case in point. A man of fine intellect, he was lost in the mists of alcoholism. His influence lay over the family like a dark shadow and affairs got so bad that eventually her mother had to have him committed to Derry Asylum.

What does Kathleen tell us about the city and the surrounding locality? Derry of a bygone era looms large with her – its characters, its sights, its sounds, the streets, the buildings, the majestic River Foyle and the countryside beyond. All are conjured up in the manner of dreamy flashbacks coming up out of the mist as they used to do in the old-time movies:

> We passed a garden where all the flowers were nodding …beyond lay the quays where I had walked with Father, where the water had plonk-plonked beneath the boards and I had to catch his hand. On the slope opposite…we saw the wall of the barracks with the toy soldiers in sentry boxes. The tiny ferryboat was pulling a silver line through the water across to the Guildhall.

Kathleen was born at 48 Abercorn Road, Derry, in 1886, into dynasties that were solidly Catholic on both sides. Her maternal great-grandfather, the redoubtable John McNulty, had helped to build the Long Tower chapel in the 1780s and was a personal friend of the Catholic bishop, Dr McDevitt, and the Protestant bishop, Frederick Hervey, Earl of Bristol. Hervey had donated £200 for the erection of the Long Tower and on visits to see the chapel's progress would delight John McNulty with colourful stories of his famous European travels. Later McNulty described Hervey as, 'a glorious scamp of a bishop and a glorious friend…' It was this John McNulty who did a most gracious thing before his marriage. When he was out walking one evening with his sweetheart she admired a damson tree that was in bloom. John purchased the ground forthwith and built a house for his bride-to-be with the damson tree sitting proudly in the middle of the garden. There's romance for you! We also learn that this beautiful damson tree was the scene of extraordinary ecumenical get-togethers when John McNulty would sit under it on summer days with Bishop McDevitt on one side and Bishop Hervey on the other, discussing the great issues of the day.

When Kathleen Coyle was only two years of age she sustained an accident to her foot – something she was reminded of for the rest of her life as she had to wear a patten (shoe platform) to avoid having a pronounced limp. It also meant that while her brother and two sisters went off to boarding school she had to remain at home, educated by a tutor and a French teacher. This was unusual for Derry Catholics and a measure of the Coyle family wealth.

Kathleen's parents, John and Catherine, were well-educated and had an extensive library. It was here that Kathleen spent most of her spare time as she grew up. She wiled away the hours reading literature and philosophy and there's little doubt that this love of books eventually led her towards the world of writing. When she was not reading she was acutely observing Derry. One lasting impression was the annual burning of the effigy of Lundy, regarded as a traitor during the city's Siege in 1689. Kathleen, aged thirteen, tells us: 'He hung in the heavens – burning like a lantern from the feet upwards.' But a bigger burning was soon to be seen when Coyle's great haberdashery store in Bishop Street went up in flames. Kathleen's father John was deemed responsible for the disaster. We are left to think that he may have been careless after an evening's drinking. Yet Kathleen cannot bring herself to blame him: 'I could accept no fault in my father...'

As John's alcoholism slowly pushes the family towards breaking point, we learn that his mother and the other Coyle in-laws have little time for his wife, Catherine. The manner in which Kathleen makes these family disclosures is very interesting. They never come from her own lips but are usually left to another character to slip in as innuendo – as with McDaid, the family driver, when Kathleen and he are looking down at the inmates in Derry Asylum from nearby Northland Road. Her father, unknown to her, is ensconced therein after a drinking binge. 'Look well, you might see somebody you know,' says McDaid mockingly. With John's life in a downward spiral, something was bound to give. Kathleen's mother removed the children from the grip of the Coyle in-laws and set up home in Belt Cottage in the Waterside.

> Something about that place embraced us from the
> beginning. It had an air of greeting, of waiting for
> us, of having expected us for a long time.

And so a new chapter opened for the virtually fatherless family, with descriptions of life in the magnificent Glendermott Valley and along the banks of the sparkling River Faughan. Then came attendance at Ardmore School. Kathleen arrived on the first day with Major, her beloved dog, two cats and two kid goats – much to the chagrin of the poor schoolmaster, who beat a hasty retreat. It turned out to be her only day at school and soon a tutor came to Belt Cottage: 'a tall thin dark young man with a beaked nose and pink face'. Kathleen took an instant dislike to him. Yet the tutor is forgotten in the magic of Christmas and attendance at Midnight Mass in St Columb's on the Waterside's Chapel Road:

> The world was silvered over with the blue quality
> of mystery...crisp roads, our steps like wooden
> notes...down the steep sharp road to the chapel.

Alongside the happiness in Kathleen Coyle's work there is a haunting melancholy, which is especially detectable in her women, with tales of lost love and of men who could not live up to expectations. Failed marriages abound. Kathleen also reminds us continually of the overbearing influence of her great-aunts – the daughters of John McNulty. John had two boys and six girls – of these Ahn (Ann) and Brigid became something of museum pieces, spinster aunts, who lived in the house with the damson tree, where time stood still:

> Ahn was a little shell of a woman who consisted mainly of clothes...Brigid was tall and stately...

When Kathleen came to call they always argued about times past but paused to serve cake and tea in delicate gold-rimmed china cups. Visits ended with a gift of money: '...a crisply new Bank of Ireland note...' and the customary cynical question:

> And Father – what is he up to now?

Another of the McNulty girls was Kathleen's grandmother Elizabeth. She had a tale to tell: a horrendous sea voyage from Derry Quay to New York and then the tragedy of a broken heart when her sister Jane refused to let her marry a handsome soldier. This Jane – 'Plain Jane McNulty' – the ugly ducking of the family, rose to be a well-loved New York personality in her own right. Jane became a close friend of Nancy Delano Astor one of the richest women in the world. So close were the pair that Nancy offered Jane an island in New York's East River as a gift. It was a priceless piece of real estate but, unbelievably, Jane turned it down, saying she was much too busy with her own work. Eventually she returned to Derry, a very wealthy woman with the grand title of Madame Watters, and henceforth devoted her life to religion and philanthropy. It is long-forgotten now but Jane erected scores of new houses and helped to fund the building of St Eugene's Cathedral, the Nazareth House and St Columb's College.

All these events occurred before Kathleen Coyle's time

and with the arrival of the 1900s her mother was finding it difficult to make ends meet at Belt Cottage. The solution was draconian: sell the cottage and move to England. And it is at this point that Kathleen leaves us, with the long, winding road into adulthood looming. She does so with a final walk through the Coyle and McNulty lands around St Eugene's Cathedral:

> Along Creggan Road Mother showed me the Bishop's (Hervey's) demesne…We saw the sweep of Clarendon Street going down towards the river (Foyle)…then the blur of low streets where the little house was with its damson tree…

These are wistful, farewell glances. Kathleen tells us that her mother made a sweeping gesture towards the Cathedral and the tiny rows of houses built by Jane:

> 'You realise, Kathleen, that this is in all of us and we cannot escape from it.'

Although the family did flee, leaving Derry for ever in 1906, Kathleen's mother was right. There was to be no escape: Derry was always in Kathleen's mind, her magical realm. And she finishes by recalling some of the precious memories she carried with her:

> *Farewell Faughan, farewell Keenaght,*
> *Farewell all for I must leave you.*
> *Farewell my hills and farewell my mountains,*
> *Farewell my plains and farewell my fountains.*
> *Farewell my road with the roses above the plain of Aileach*
> *Roses that caught in my hair as a child.*

from Charles Gallagher, *Acorns and Oak Leaves – A Derry Childhood*

One afternoon – it was a Saturday – in May 1932 I was walking home from my aunt's house in Miller Street, when I heard the unmistakable sound of an aeroplane engine. It wasn't the deep sonorous roar of the RAF flying boats but a lighter, high-pitched sound. I gazed skywards and then I saw it – a little red monoplane. Because of my boyish interest in flying I knew what a Gypsy Moth or a Bristol Bulldog looked like and I was familiar with the shape of the Vickers Virginia bombers but this was different and puzzling. Swiftly it sped across the sky, banked over the Waterside and slanted down towards Pennyburn. I didn't realise it but I was witnessing the final stage of one of the most dramatic of all transatlantic flights – the first solo crossing by a woman pilot – Amelia Earhart.

Amelia's Plane was a Lockheed Viga and is now in the Smithsonian Museum in Washington. The flight took fourteen hours and fifty-six minutes. Amelia had followed the railway track from the coast to Derry and, with fuel almost exhausted, had to find a landing. Eventually she did land on a sloping field at Ballyarnett, just outside the city, despite the fact that one of her landing wheels struck a branch of a tall tree at McGeadys' house on the descent. James McGeady, one of the first people to reach the plane, thought the oil-spattered pilot was a young man. Amelia's first words are said to have been: 'Can you tell me where I am?'

CURIOSITIES

The Tale of the Vanishing Lover

There is a castle at Liscloon,
Where lovers met and souls entwined,
Only to leave a memory,
A tragedy in parting.
Whispers the wind across the hill.
A dying gust, an eerie chill.
'Tis silent now under the moon,
The empty castle at Liscloon

Was the bond of love strong enough for him to return and claim the woman he loved? The gaunt and menacing-looking ruin of a castle outside Donemana, County Tyrone, holds a grim secret. It was here that the lord of the manor fell in love with a village girl, only to vanish suddenly and leave her heartbroken. Rumour had it that he was banished from Ireland by his family and had found fame as a scientist overseas. But...

Picture this: a morning in early summer on the height above Donemana that gives you a view into Derry and the great sweep of the river Foyle beyond. Northwards you can see the hills of Inishowen and far away on the horizon in west Donegal are the craggy outlines of Muckish and Errigal. It truly is a magical setting and it was here in the late 1870s that Mary Jane Jamieson met James Ogilby in what turned out to be a most fateful encounter. She was sixteen years of age and he was twenty-seven. The exact spot is said to have been Curryfree – 'the heathery hill'. The girl was the daughter of a local farmer, while the young man was the second son of the

Ogilbys of Altnacree Castle at Liscloon, outside Donemana. Fittingly enough Altnacree means 'hill of my heart'.

Mary Jane Jamieson was carrying silk embroidered shirts into Derry when James Ogilby asked if he could accompany her along the way. At first sight it would seem to have been an odd pairing: she a poor seamstress and he rich and well-educated. He had spent his preparatory years at St Columba's College in Dublin, then went to the famous English public school, Winchester, where he distinguished himself as a footballer and cricketer. At the age of sixteen he was selected to play for the Winchester first eleven in cricket and regularly turned in brilliant batting performances. The family ran into hard times financially in 1869 and to his great sadness James was withdrawn from Winchester. We next find him attending Trinity College Dublin, where he studied zoology with great success. While at Trinity he took up athletics and in one of his many races defeated the Irish champion of the time.

James Ogilby had one brother and five sisters. Although he was helping to manage the Liscloon estate he really wanted to continue his profession as a zoologist abroad. He had worked in the British Museum and was at that time engaged in researching fish stocks in the river Foyle.

Despite the disparity in the situation of the young people, it appears that the farmer's daughter was well taught at her grandmother's knee and could converse with anyone. Added to this she had the looks of a true Irish beauty, with fine features and magnificent auburn hair.

All we know of that fateful morning is that the minute the pair set eyes on each other they fell head over heels in love. Thereafter they met in secret every day, favourite spots being Altnacree glen and the nearby Dennet burn. Tradition also holds that they passed love notes to each other by way of an owl's nest in an old oak tree. But there was a problem for the lovers: James's mother Adelaide ruled with a rod of iron and she had her own plans for the Ogilby children. Her idea was that the boys would marry girls with big dowries, while the girls would set their sights on the richest men in the land. So coachloads of possibles rolled up to Altnacree Castle for dances and soirées under the watchful eye of Mama Ogilby. Imagine then her fury, when the young couple announced that they wanted to marry and travel the world and that nothing would change their minds. Quite simply it was something she would not tolerate. The lovers must be separated. Immediately she devised a cunning plan to cool her son's ardour.

Firstly, James was dispatched to relations of the Ogilbys in County Cavan on the pretext of urgent business. Actually there is a version of the story that says he was packed off against his will. Whatever the truth of this, Mama Ogilby then played her trump card. Realising that James had a passion for zoology and dreamed of going to America, she offered to pay for his expenses if he would go there immediately. As for Mary Jane, he could pen a letter to the girl explaining that arrangements would be made for her later. To help James to make up his mind his mother further added that under no circumstances would he be permitted to return to Donemana or Liscloon in the foreseeable future. In effect, in that year, 1882 he was banished from Ireland.

Meanwhile, back in Donemana, Mary Jane knew nothing of her sweetheart's whereabouts. As far as she was concerned he had suddenly vanished from the face of the earth. If James wrote a letter she never received it. In fact no explanation was ever given for his disappearance. As you might guess, the effect on the girl was devastating. She packed her wedding dress away and thereafter was seen wandering about Donemana in what can only be described as a state of mourning. Over the years she might be spotted along the Dennet burn, pining away from a broken heart. It seemed as if her beloved had gone for ever.

Then came an amazing twist in the tale. Out of the blue, in the autumn of 1884, James Ogilby turned up once more in Donemana and despite his mama's objections, claimed the hand of the overjoyed Mary Jane Jamieson. It was said that she first got word of his return when she discovered a note from him in the old owl's nest tree. The pair married in Earlsgift Church in the village and straight away departed for Australia, never to return. James made a brilliant career for himself in zoology, firstly in the Sydney Museum and later in the Queensland Museum. But it was not to be a fairytale ending, for the sweethearts had only a short life together. Mary Jane fell ill with TB and died in 1893 at the age of twenty-nine. Sadly, the couple had no family and James never married again. Worse still, he had a growing addiction to alcohol and this eventually brought a halt to his blossoming scientific career. However, he had already published several books and significant works on marine species, so his name became famous in the annals of zoology.

James Ogilby died in Brisbane in 1925 at the age of seventy-two, a victim of loneliness and heavy drinking, eminent in Australia but forgotten in his homeland. His friends said he often reminisced about his boyhood days at Liscloon and Donemana. Most of all he would recall how he had met his sweetheart, Mary Jane Jamieson, on the slopes of Altnacree.

Where did James Ogilby disappear to in 1882? Recent research has enabled us to trace Ogilby's movements after he was banished from Donemana. From Cavan he travelled to the eastern seaboard of America. He then journeyed to Texas, where he began to research bird life in Navarro County. Here he made an outstanding contribution to the cataloguing of birds in the region. While still in America he applied for the post of zoology curator in the Sydney Museum, Australia, and was successful in his application. This prompted him to make the hasty return to Donemana in the autumn of 1884 that was much to the delight of his sweetheart Mary Jane Jamieson.

James and Mary Jane were married on 24 November 1884 and then left for Sydney, arriving in February 1885. By 1887 James Ogilby had achieved fame through his research into fish in the seas off Australia and was accepted into the distinguished Linnean Society of London. Despite his prodigious work, he was dismissed from the Sydney Museum in 1890 for excessive drinking. However, the Queensland Museum, Brisbane, recruited James and by 1903 he was carrying out research on the marine life around Australia's Gold Coast.

James Ogilby was frequently censured for his drinking but such was his outstanding contribution to zoology that he was given a special room in the Queensland Museum where he could come and go as he pleased, regardless of his alcoholic state. Finally, the prestigious Amateur Fisherman's Association of Queensland elected him a life member and upon his death in 1925 set up the J.D. Ogilby Memorial Cottage Museum in his memory on Bribie Island near Brisbane.

The story of James Ogilby prompted much interest over the past few years and eventually reached Australian shores. In the summer of 2003, knowing that she had an Ogilby connection, Mrs Joy Ware came from Australia to visit the ruins of Altnacree Castle at Donemana. Joy discovered that James Ogilby's eldest sister, Adelaide Charlotte, was her great-grandmother and now hopes to write a book on the Ogilby saga.

Back in 1924, James Ogilby had written his own autobiography. This was just a year before he died in Australia. In the manuscript, which is unfinished but entitled *The Early Years of a Naturalist*, he talks of his boyhood days in Donemana and records details of the wildlife that so much took his interest. He also describes what day-to-day life was like in Altnacree Castle and gives us an invaluable memoir of the local countryside in the 1860s.

Unfortunately the manuscript breaks off just before James met Mary Jane Jamieson. We shall never know the exact details of the dealings with his stern mother that led to his banishment from Liscloon and the castle on the Altnacree.

from James Douglas Ogilby,
The Early Years of a Naturalist (1925)

A gateway from the castle stable yard led to a
sheltered lane of brambles and bracken that was a
favourite haunt for us children. Here in springtime
were to be found the first primroses and dog-
violets of the opening year, and now here in autumn
did such large and lustrous blackberries grow.
At the lane's end it entered the steep cross-roads,
which united the upper and lower roads to Derry. I
recall a plantation of evergreen trees, spruce, larch
and pine, which was the reputed abiding place of
fairies and leprechauns and was therefore held in
high honour and no little awe by us.

Tom Thumb and the Derry Giant

The Rise and Fall of Jimmy Allender

Everybody agreed; it was a sensation! Tom Thumb, the smallest man on earth, cavorting on stage with Jimmy Allender, Derry's gentle giant. Nothing like it had ever been seen before and it had the city at fever pitch in the early 1870s. As a result Jimmy Allender set out from Derry on the road to stardom, a journey that would take him halfway round the globe and back again and in the end leave him totally destitute.

Back in the Derry of the 1870s there was one thing they said about Jimmy Allender – you could spot him a mile away. In crowds, in parades, on market days or other big events, Jimmy stood head and shoulders above everybody because he was eight feet tall; most likely he was the tallest man in Ireland. A hundred years earlier Patrick Cotter had established the all-time record at a height of almost nine feet and became famous as 'The Giant O'Brien'.

Jimmy was an orphan, brought up in Gwyn's Institution, which was originally situated in Derry's Brooke Park and built to house poor children. There he trained to be a tailor and by his late teens was able to provide a living for himself, meagre as it was. But things were about to change for the gentle giant, as he was known, thanks to a remarkable set of circumstances.

It happened that Charles Stratton, alias 'General' Tom Thumb, the world's smallest man, came to Derry as part of his world tour. Tom had taken the title 'General' to add a bit of flourish to his stage show. He was barely three feet tall and his wife Lavinia, who also took part in the entertainment, was smaller still. Tom Thumb and his performers, mostly small people with a variety of talents, were billed to appear in Derry's Corporation Hall in the Diamond. It was here that J.F. Warden, an actor and promoter, introduced Jimmy Allender to Tom. Warden had the bright idea that Jimmy would be Gulliver, the giant in the land of the Lilliputians, played by Tom and his retinue of little people. So Swift's famous novel, *Gulliver's Travels*, would be played out in reality on the Derry stage.

It has to be said that these were days when fairgrounds, sideshows and museums often displayed curiosities that would offend today's sensibilities. Five-legged cows and bearded ladies were commonplace and usually bogus. It was into this arena that the famous showman Phineas T. Barnum had introduced Charles Stratton as Tom Thumb in 1842; his first exhibition was alongside a lady known as the Fiji Mermaid. Tom went from success to success and became a very rich man. He made several round-the-world trips and was in his late thirties when he arrived in Derry.

On the eve of the first north-west performance news swept through town that a horse-drawn van had arrived in the Diamond with Tom Thumb's magnificent coach. People said it was little bigger than a doll's house and was drawn by tiny white ponies. The show itself commenced with a mixture of singing and sketches, Lavinia, Tom's wife, being much to the fore. Then came the lordly arrival of Tom in the famous coach, flanked by a guard of honour. So the night went on until the last scene – the pièce de résistance. The curtain went back to reveal Derry's own Jimmy Allender supine and bound on the stage, a prisoner of Tom Thumb's mocking Lilliputians, who were jeering and dancing around him. At a given signal Jimmy suddenly broke free from his bindings and scattered his captors to the four ends of the hall. It had the audience rolling in the aisles with laughter and the chase went on for ages with the place in absolute uproar.

As you might guess, the show was the talk of Derry the

following day. Jimmy Allender, the gentle giant, had become a star overnight and it whetted his appetite for showbusiness. Of course there was little occupation for him locally so in the mid-1870s he decided to try his luck in America, where, he heard, there was a vast array of circus sideshows. It's believed that he travelled out of Derry Quay on the great sailing vessel *Minnehaha* – perhaps her last passenger sailing. He had in his pocket a letter of introduction from J.F. Warden to a fellow-promoter at the Centennial Exhibition in Philadelphia and this got him his first booking. In truth the days of the sideshows were numbered; even P.T. Barnum, the greatest of the American showmen, had moved on to develop his world famous Barnum and Bailey Circus. Inevitably Jimmy Allender was not able to find enough bookings and was soon eking out a miserable existence. In the end he decided to make for the Great Exhibition of Paris in 1878, where he billed himself *Le Géant Irlandais*. Unfortunately he was relegated to the periphery of the proceedings and once more business was poor. It seemed that Jimmy's bid for stardom was failing fast.

The next we hear of Jimmy is that he had joined a travelling fair touring England. As you can imagine he was as poor as ever but by then he also had a wife and two children to support. When he was in his mid-thirties his health began to fail and soon he was unable to earn anything as a sideshow exhibit. Jimmy's final act came with his entry to the South Shields Workhouse in England – a brand new building for the destitute opened in 1880.

Jimmy was not to enjoy the frugal comforts offered to the inmates for very long for he was dead within a year. He was thirty-eight years of age and had been on the road as a sideshow exhibit for just six years. Three years later, Tom Thumb, the man who had started Jimmy's career in Derry's Corporation Hall, died of a stroke at the age of forty-six. Lavinia, his wife remarried, an Italian, Count Magri, and thereafter styled herself as Countess Magri, living to the age of seventy-seven.

At least, Jimmy Allender escaped the fate of his earlier rival, 'The Giant O'Brien'. During his life O'Brien was hounded by anatomists, who wanted to dissect him when he died; he was followed everywhere. Eventually he left instructions that after his death he was to be buried in twelve feet of solid rock, secured by iron bars. It was to no avail. In 1972 his body was exhumed and very detail photographed for the entire world to see.

Tom Thumb was not the first tiny man to stage a show in Derry. Eighty years earlier, in 1796, Count Boralosky from Poland came to a local hotel and announced himself as the smallest man in the world – he was less than three feet tall and almost sixty years of age. A Frenchman touring Ireland in 1796 reported that he had encountered the count in Derry, accompanied by his wife, who was of normal height. Apparently Boralosky could speak five languages and was an accomplished musician.

However, it was not all plain sailing. One day, the Count, who had a high-pitched voice, had a dispute with his wife and refused to stop complaining. Eventually the poor woman could take no more, so she lifted the little man and set him high up on the mantelpiece, where he kicked his heels. He had earlier achieved fame in London, when he teamed up with the Giant O'Brien in a forerunner of the show staged in Derry many decades later. O'Brien, short of nine feet, had everyone gasping when he produced Count Boralosky from an inside pocket and perched him on the palm of his hand.

from De Latocnaye, *Tour of Ireland* (1796)

When I was in Londonderry there was exhibiting himself a Polish dwarf who called himself Count Boraloski. He may have been two and a half feet high. This is a most extraordinary little being. He speaks four or five languages and has been very well brought up. His age is put down as between fifty and sixty years. It is said that his wife, who is of ordinary stature, in a matrimonial quarrel, one day lifted him and set him on the mantelpiece to cool his heels.

The Strabane Fleet

When Tall Ships Sailed from Derry to Strabane

Picture the scene: elegant sailing ships – schooners, clippers, and even full-rigged vessels – gliding majestically on the River Foyle en route from Derry Quay to Strabane and sometimes far beyond.. That's the way it was, back in the 1800s, when tall ships were able to berth right in the heart of the Tyrone town. Local folk would crowd the quays to marvel at the sight of the beautiful sea-going vessels. Nowadays all that remains are one or two old warehouses.

In those bygone times Strabane was one of the busiest places in Ireland, with massive cross-channel trade. Foodstuffs such as beef, pork, grain and poultry went to ports like Glasgow and Liverpool, while imports included timber, iron and general merchandise. But how did the sailing ships manage to get into Strabane in the first place? In truth it was something of a minor miracle and really all down to a fantastic feat of engineering – the Strabane Canal.

The canal was the brainchild of the Marquis of Abercorn and opened in 1796. It was just over four miles long and met the River Foyle ten miles from Londonderry at Leck, near the village of Ballymagorry. There were two locks known as Crampsie's and Devine's, so named because of families associated with them. Each was a hundred feet in length and could accommodate sailing ships up to three hundred tons.

Strabane soon became a hive of activity, especially at Canal Basin, where the new waterway terminated. You can imagine it: horses on the towpath and craft of every shape and size coming and going all day long. Men were busy at the lock gates and swing bridges and hundreds were occupied loading and unloading produce at the wharfs. Samuel Lewis tells us in his *Topographical Dictionary of Ireland* (1837) that there were: '... stores for grain, warehouses, and commodious quays, for the extensive trade...'

So business was booming and there were jobs aplenty, with the town having the air of a thriving seaport. The whole scene became even more colourful when barges were introduced to take supplies from Derry Quay. The armada of vessels towed by steam tugs inevitably found a place in local folklore as 'the Strabane fleet'. Colonel Thomas Colby's *Ordnance Survey of the County Londonderry* (1837) records the staggering figure of five hundred and eighty-three barges, with employment for a thousand men.

However, the canal was dealt two crippling blows in the mid-1800s. Firstly, there was the arrival of the Londonderry and Enniskillen Railway in 1847, bringing fierce competition. Secondly came the opening of the new iron bridge across the Foyle in 1863. From then on only vessels with low masts or funnels could get up-river. This sounded the death knell for the big schooners.

Gallantly the Strabane fleet kept the canal alive for the next seventy years by transporting sand, gravel and other bulky items not suitable for rail. And this despite the opening of the County Donegal railway terminus in the Waterside in 1900. The antics of the 'fleet' became a day-to-day talking point in the north-west in times when there was neither radio nor television. And as you might guess there were many larger-than-life characters, not to mention some mighty adventures. Top of the list is the yarn about the steam tug *Shamrock*, which hit a storm out of Derry in the early 1900s. The episode found fame in a song entitled 'The Strabane Fleet', with the opening lines setting the tone for what has become one of our great local legends.

Come all you jolly seamen bold
That plough the raging main.
Give an ear unto my story;
I'll relate to you the same.
Our Shamrock boat moved slowly off
From Derry we did go
An' at 6 o'clock that very night
The stormy winds did blow.

A night to remember it turned out to be. Mountainous waves and gale-force winds lashed the little tug near Prehen, just a little up-river from Derry. She pitched and rolled precariously for hours, in danger of capsizing at any moment. But there was a happy ending, for the heroic crew members kept their nerve and in the end made it home to Strabane.

But other storm clouds were appearing. There was now a railway on each side of the river and also transport by road so river traffic was dwindling. The end came in 1932 when the Strabane and Foyle Navigation Company ceased commercial trading. Incidentally, they were the fourth company to manage the undertaking since 1796. As you might expect, the Strabane Canal became a sorry sight over the succeeding decades. Gradually the water level fell – to less than two feet in places. Then it began to silt up and soon the locks and swing bridges fell into disrepair. But in a strange and entertaining way there was a little lease of life in 1947. That year the north-west saw one of the worst winters in living memory. The canal was solidly frozen over for five weeks. This was a cue for the ice skaters to come out and for a while there was a spectacle more like you'd find in Holland than in our milder climes.

Sad to relate, the Strabane Canal was officially abandoned in 1962. Yet even to this day the main body of the famous waterway is there for all to see alongside the River Foyle between Ballymagorry and the town. And the good news is that the restoration of the canal is still very much a talking point in Strabane. Happily this has led to progress and recently part of the locks system where the canal enters the River Foyle was beautifully restored.

Maybe it's just a dream – who knows – but perhaps one day the famous last lines of the song about the Strabane fleet song might come to pass once more.

When looking over Derry Bridge
There is nothing half so grand,
As to view the fleet that sails the deep
From Derry to Strabane.

ISLANDS IN THE FOYLE

My dream is of an island place
A little island on whose face
The stars are watchers only...
              Elizabeth Barrett Browning (*c.* 1838)

For me there's something magical about an island. Maybe it goes back to schooldays and Stevenson's *Treasure Island*, that whole idea of sailing ships and buried treasure – mystery, adventure, intrigue. Whatever the case, I was delighted on my rambles along the banks of the River Foyle to come upon two islands – Corkan Island and Island More. They are close to Port Hall, in the parish of Clonleigh, just a mile or two down-river from the towns of Strabane and Lifford. Talking of treasure, as far as I know there is none on these islands but there is a wealth of history hereabouts and some great stories to be told.

The islands lie in the middle of the river, which is really part of the greater Foyle system. Amazing to relate, there are nine hundred miles of rivers and streams in this system. It drains the Sperrin Mountains in the east and the Bluestack Mountains (Donegal) in the west to create the River Foyle at the meeting of the rivers Mourne and Finn between Strabane and Lifford. With such an influx of water at this confluence it is no surprise that the Foyle is so wide – it is also tidal and fast-flowing. Derry is about a dozen miles from here.

Corkan Island and Island More cover a distance of about three miles and appear to have been created in earlier times when part of the river broke away, leaving a narrow strip of land with a stream on either side. And while I have called them 'islands', some might argue that they should really be regarded as one island, since nothing more than a drain separates the two. They are low-lying and quite irregular in shape and taper out considerably as the river moves northwards towards Derry. As regards the origin of the names of the islands I could get no clear information on this locally. Island More speaks for itself – 'Big Island' and Corkan is close to Corcoran – an Irish family name possibly contracted from Mac Corcrain, a corrupted form of Mac Corcurain (Corcuran's son), where *corcur* may mean purple. Or the name could come from the shape of the island; another Irish dictionary derivation gives corcan as 'pot' or 'pot-bellied'.

An old railway bridge at Port Hall, which is on the Foyle's left bank, provides access to Corkan Island. This is the only means of getting on to the islands by land, as it were. It is also a reminder that the Great Northern Railway route from Derry to Belfast and Dublin came this way until it was closed in 1965. The metal railway bridge, locally named Port Hall Bridge, appears to be as solid now as when it was built in the 1860s – a wonderful piece of Victorian engineering. The railway crossed from Donegal on the left bank of the river on to Corkan Island and met a similar bridge on the other side of the island, taking it across to Northern Ireland and on to Strabane. This latter bridge – known as McKinney's Bridge – was dismantled several decades ago, leaving only the stout iron pillars sitting in the river. It is a spectacular sight.

So what can we discover about the islands in the Foyle? Delving into the records, I find that this was a much busier place from the mid-1800s to the early 1900s. Port Hall itself was a station on the line and as well as the trains coming and going to Derry all day long, the Foyle and Bann Fisheries Company had a base here for the netting of salmon. Sand and gravel were also taken from the river but the main activity on the islands was farming. In 1911 there was a large house on Corkan Island with ten occupants and a substantial farm.

One impressive aspect of this farming household was that seven of the eight children were still at school – the eldest aged eighteen. That year of 1911 would have produced a bumper harvest on the islands for it was a beautiful summer – the warmest in living memory. In Derry it was so dry that they talked of a 'water famine'. How different it has been since then, especially in the years following the Millennium. Successive wet summers left Corkan Island and Island More so severely flooded at times that you would think the river was trying to claim them back.

Chatting with local people, I came upon two intriguing tales about the islands. The first concerns territorial jurisdiction. When the Irish Free State was formed in 1922 a new feature came into being, the border with Northern Ireland. The remit for deciding where the border actually lay was given to the Border Commission, appointed in 1924. Controversy reigned then and in some ways probably still does. By way of example, in this part of the world the river was seen as a natural boundary so a line was drawn down the centre of the River Foyle, leaving the right bank in Northern Ireland and the left (Donegal) bank in the Free State. Hardly had this been agreed when it was discovered that the new border would run through the centre of Corkan Island and Island More. So were they in the North or were they in the South with regard to jurisdiction? The plain fact was that no one could decide.

Then someone in the Border Commission had a bright, almost surreal idea. They would float a barrel down the river from Lifford Bridge and whichever side it was washed in at would determine the nationality of the islands. Curious onlookers duly assembled on the bridge and saw the sealed barrel launched into the river. It held its course in midstream for what seemed like ages before going with this current and that (the gods were deliberating) but then slowly and surely the barrel was seen to drift to the Donegal bank where it eventually came to a halt.

Thus did fate decide the nationality of Corkan Island

and Island More. They were to be part of what was later to be known as the Republic of Ireland. As you might guess, the wisdom of such a method of determination was a source of much debate: what would have happened if the river had been in flood and the barrel washed downstream to the sea, as one wiseacre joked? Or what if the river had been too low for the barrel to go anywhere, asked another? On and on the questions went. It was all part of the cut and thrust but in the end purely hypothetical – subsequent Ordnance Survey maps showed the islands within the domain of southern Ireland and its government. It was however an extraordinary episode and a tribute to local folklore that it can still be recalled.

The second tale involves hare coursing, of which there has been a long tradition in and around the Lifford area, as in many parts of Ireland. It is a topic of immense controversy. However, the story goes that in times past when coursing flourished hereabouts, hares were netted and kept on the islands in the Foyle. It also appears that hare-netting became something of an industry, as the captive hares from here were exported all over Ireland. At first I thought these hares must have been allowed to roam as they pleased on the islands but then I remembered that they could have escaped by crossing either of the two railway bridges. So they must have been fenced in, perhaps with water on each side. No sign of that any more: in fact very little sign of hares of either breed – Irish or brown. But if any do appear I hope they enjoy more freedom that their poor forebears, who were prisoners on the islands in the Foyle in former times.

Finally to a man who fell in love with Corkan Island and Island More – the colourful and talented Anthony (Tony) Marreco. Tony came to Ireland in the 1950s and took up residence in Port Hall, an elegant Georgian house that had been designed by the Derry architect, Michael Priestley, for the Vaughan family in 1746. Marreco was a larger-than-life character – famed for his liaisons with some of the world's most beautiful women. His good looks and charm were said to melt the hearts of the fair sex. He was married four times, his last marriage being to his former second wife. In his time Tony Marreco was an actor, a barrister, a naval officer and a British diplomat in Germany after the Second World War. He was also a much-travelled man. Among his many claims to fame was that he was a member of the British delegation at the Nuremburg Trials. Later, he became one of the founding members of Amnesty International. Those who met him recall that he was a brilliant raconteur and a man of great conviviality.

Despite his colourful lifestyle Tony was captivated by the River Foyle and the local countryside – which brings us to the islands. He loved nothing more than to wander about them and view the River Foyle in all its moods. He also loved the spectacular rolling countryside hereabouts. Did he ponder his great adventures and liaisons, I wonder? Did he need the solitude of these surroundings to make sense of it all? Tony had met Gandhi and Lawrence of Arabia while a pupil at Westminster School and had known Rudolf Hess and Hermann Göring, amongst other war criminals of the Second World War. Last and certainly by no means least, his breath-taking trysts would outdo a library of romantic novels. In Shakespeare's *The Tempest*, Caliban says, 'The isle is full of noises, Sounds and sweet airs that give delight…'

Tony Marreco died in 2006, at the age of ninety. It would be nice to think that his spirit visits Corkan Island and Island More from time to time, bringing what the Bard describes so eloquently and even, perhaps, endowing the place with some of his own special Marreco magic.

Gilfillan's Weird Secret

Wood of Life

An ancient graveyard at Enagh Lough just outside Derry holds a mystery. Here, in an overgrown plot, lies at rest a local surgeon who sailed the seas with a world-famous explorer but returned to Derry a broken man. Strange to relate, on one of his voyages he learned something that he would never reveal to anyone and in the end he literally took his secret to the grave. But now, after years of research, clues have been uncovered that might hold the key to one of the north-west's great riddles.

On a balmy July afternoon in the year 1830 there was the usual frenzy as a newly arrived cross-channel schooner tied up at the quayside in Derry. Curious onlookers eyed those disembarking and saw one man who stood out above the others. He was tall, rather haggard-looking, moved with difficulty and, despite the pleasant weather he wore a top hat, a scarf and greatcoat. Strange as this was, his most distinguishing feature was the black patch over one eye. Undoubtedly it lent a sinister air to that Foyleside scene.

The traveller was thirty-seven-year-old Alexander Gilfillan, a naval surgeon, who had returned to Derry after years at sea. Indeed, to be more precise, he was on his way to his father's home at Gorticross, just a few miles from the city. It did not take a genius to see that Gilfillan was ill – his drawn look and pale complexion were testament to that. As if to prove the point, he snapped impatiently at the deck hands dealing with his luggage, a surgeon's trunk and an odd-looking bundle of deep-brown wooden planks, which appeared to be very heavy.

The trunk, containing medical instruments, was of course his stock-in-trade. As for the wood, as we shall see it was to be put to a more macabre use after his death, although it was to be another eight years before the Grim Reaper came calling at Gilfillan's door. In this time, he would marry, see great tragedy in his family and make a chilling prophecy about the nature of his demise.

For clues to this strange tale we have to visit the leafy little graveyard of Enagh in Judge's Road, a couple of miles outside Derry. Here a large gravestone records that this is Alexander Gilfillan's last resting-place: died 27 March 1838, aged forty-five years. But what follows really catches the eye, for the reader is informed that Gilfillan sailed as a surgeon with the great Sir John Franklin on his voyage of discovery to the Arctic. A further rather curious line adds that Alexander Gilfillan died at Gorticross on the same day as his father, Joseph

How did Gilfillan come to sail with Franklin, who was without doubt one of the world's most famous explorers? It's a gripping story of a boy's ambition to become a naval doctor and travel the world. And while Alexander did have a measure of success in his life, in the end all he had to show for it was bitterness and a strange preoccupation with death.

Alexander Gilfillan was born at Gorticross in 1793, the youngest son of a farmer, Joseph Gilfillan, whose forebears were Scottish. At the age of fifteen he persuaded his parents to let him take up Latin lessons with the hope of eventually becoming a doctor. He was later to recall his sheer delight in running down through the fields to cross the River Faughan on the way to his teacher's house. By 1813 Alexander had completed initial medical training and joined the Royal Navy with the rank of assistant surgeon. Apparently he was a very striking young man – tall and good-looking, with a ruddy complexion and a shock of curly black hair. One drawback was his quick temper – a Gilfillan trait – and with his irascible nature Alexander did not suffer fools gladly. Yet he proved to be an excellent doctor and within a few years his medical skills were impressing his navy bosses. As a reward, in 1818, they offered him the post of assistant surgeon on HMS *Trent*, which was to undertake a great voyage of discovery to the North Pole. The *Trent* was to be commanded by the famous explorer, Sir John Franklin, in company with another vessel, the HMS *Dorothea*.

For an obscure surgeon like Gilfillan the honour of sailing with Franklin and the chance of being one of the first men to reach the Pole was a dream come true. Earlier voyages had failed but hopes were high on this occasion, as both the *Trent* and the *Dorothea* had specially strengthened hulls to cope with the ice that had been found to be a major hazard on previous trips.

Unfortunately the expedition turned out to be a catastrophe. Both vessels were almost wrecked near the Arctic Circle in a series of massive ice storms; indeed the *Dorothea* was reduced to a leaking hulk. To make matters worse Gilfillan himself began to lose his sight due to snow-blindness, a condition little understood in those early days. And while some vision returned, initial reports indicated that his eyes were irreparably damaged.

If Alexander Gilfillan's star had until then been in the ascendant, suddenly it was rapidly fading. It seems that from then on his life saw nothing but misfortune. True, he was appointed to the rank of full surgeon in 1822 at the age of twenty-nine. Yet he was barely in the post when the sight went permanently from one eye. Following this the navy temporarily invalided him out on half-pay and reluctantly he made his way home to Gorticross to recuperate. It was here that he had the idea of applying for a full discharge from the navy, probably in the hope that he could practise medicine locally and also have a pension.

It was a plan that didn't work. Alexander Gilfillan was forced to attend countless medical examinations, with most reports maintaining that his remaining eye was still in good enough condition. He fumed about his treatment and soon the fiery Gilfillan temper reached breaking point and Alexander made an open attack on his navy masters. Still they refused to release him and in a rather cynical move in November 1827 posted him to the Naval Hospital in Kingston, Jamaica, in the West Indies – virtually the end of the world for a navy man. It was a real banishment to the colonies, a dead-end location. He spent two miserable years in Jamaica, a broody, disillusioned character with a patch over his damaged eye. Often his fellow officers chided him for refusing to take alcohol but in time, like many others, he became addicted to drink. In the end his health broke down completely and all too late the navy released him. By now he was an alcoholic and a shadow of his former self.

This then was the Alexander Gilfillan who alighted on Derry Quay in that summer of 1830, after his journey from the West Indies. About a year later, at the age of thirty-seven, he married Elizabeth McCutcheon, the daughter of a local farmer. Their happiness was short-lived, for their first child Joseph was scalded to death at three years of age when a pot of boiling water tipped over him. This accident was never fully explained but it had a devastating effect on the former doctor, whose drinking was now out of control. On the odd day he was sober he would recall his days on the high seas – the great times with Sir John Franklin and the astonishing sights in the northern wastes beyond the Arctic Circle.

Gradually his intemperate ways took their toll. While his wife Elizabeth continued to manage the home patiently, the ageing father, Joseph, condemned his son's behaviour outright. The story goes that one day after his father had chided him, Gilfillan, now deeply depressed and preoccupied with death, roared back angrily, 'Listen, old man! You see that white horse out there in the farmyard? One day soon it will draw both our coffins to the graveyard!' Gilfillan's bizarre prophecy came true. Father and son died on the same day and were buried together on the same day – and the white horse did indeed draw them to Enagh graveyard. Incidentally, Joseph Gilfillan died in the morning and Alexander in the afternoon of 27 March 1838.

It is in connection with his death that one intriguing mystery still surrounds Gilfillan. Not long before he died, whether by premonition or otherwise, he summoned the local carpenter to his barn and instructed him to make a coffin from the bundle of wooden planks he had brought back from Jamaica eight years earlier. It seems the wood was so hard the task took weeks; the poor carpenter said he hadn't seen anything like it in all his years. In reply Gilfillan's only comment was that the wood was very special and carried a secret he would not reveal. Eventually the newly-made coffin got pride of place in the barn – an eerie sight indeed, as was the presence of the morose Gilfillan, who frequently came to gloat over it.

What was Gilfillan's secret? From research we now know that the wood he brought back from Jamaica was *lignum vitae* – quite literally the wood of life. It is a rare wood mainly native to the West Indies but also grows in parts of Florida in the form of a bush. Amongst other qualities *lignum vitae* was valued in past times for its durability. Probably the toughest wood known, it is so dense it will not float and so hard it can be used for engine parts. Alexander Gilfillan had heard of the merits of *lignum vitae* while in the West Indies and, being a doctor, had learned other things about it. For example, it is believed to have many curative qualities. It is also highly aromatic and is self-preserving as it continually exudes a heavy oil. Water will not penetrate this amazing wood.

Since Gilfillan chose a coffin of *lignum vitae* we must assume that for some reason he wanted to be buried in a watertight casket, perhaps with some sort of embalming effect. Why this should be we shall never know, for this is the secret he took to his grave. In an odd way, many years after his death, there was a progress report on the state of Alexander Gilfillan's coffin. When his wife Elizabeth died, almost sixty years later, the Enagh grave was opened once more. Alexander's son, Joseph, (born posthumously and called after the child who had died from scalding) found himself looking down at his father's coffin and was taken aback by what he saw. It was in magnificent condition – 'as new as the day it went in', was the description – not a blemish, not the slightest sign of any decay, clean and bright-looking, just as if it had been interred that very instant.

AFTERWORD: FRANKLIN'S STRANGE DERRY CONNECTION

It turns out that the famous explorer Sir John Franklin has a connection with Derry besides Alexander Gilfillan. In the summer of 1845 Franklin set out for the icy northern latitudes in search of the North-West Passage. This trip was to see the loss of all hands, including Franklin, in the ships *Erebus* and *Terror*. The story is legendary and lives on today.

At the time, a two-year search for the explorers proved fruitless and all hope was given up until a Derryman announced that he knew where Franklin was. This was Captain William Coppin, the shipbuilder, who lived at Ivy House on the city's Strand Road. Coppin, a much-respected citizen, claimed that the ghost of his recently deceased young daughter Louisa, aged almost four, had appeared to him and revealed Franklin's whereabouts. So convinced was he that he travelled to Lady Franklin to offer encouragement for another search. This eventually did take place and, odd to relate, the remains of the expedition were found in the place that the child had indicated.

The Case of the Disappearing Colonel

Derry holds some incredible stories and none more so than the amazing tale of Colonel George Knox, the last of the famous local family to live at Prehen, who executed what can only be called a remarkable vanishing trick. Prehen House, overlooking the River Foyle from the Waterside, is a remarkable dwelling. On the outside it has a plain Georgian façade but inside a warm, welcoming atmosphere awaits you. Built by Andrew Knox back in 1740, it's a much lived-in place that's now been beautifully restored by the Peck family. But there's also a touch of melancholy in the air hereabouts for the tragedy of Mary Ann Knox, shot by her lover John McNaghten, had its roots within these walls.

Born in 1832, George Knox spent his early childhood at Prehen and was a bright, lively, good-looking lad. From the outset he was brought up on tales of adventure. His father Andrew had fought at the battle of Waterloo (18 June 1815), then spent years in the Punjab in the early days of the Raj. It's hardly a surprise then that George Knox was imbued with wanderlust. As a child there was nothing he liked more than exploring the woods of Prehen, where the trees were said to be the last links with the ancient oaks of Derry. The word Prehen (from the Irish *préachán*) means 'Place of the crows'.

The Knox estate stretched all the way to New Buildings village, a distance of three miles, and the Colonel later used to recall an extraordinary meeting he had when he was about ten years old. One day he came upon the cottage of a former Knox family servant, the one-hundred-year-old David McCullagh, who had been a member of the coach party when Mary Ann

Knox was murdered in November 1761. Amazingly the old man was able to recount details of the tragedy that had happened eighty years earlier – and which is recalled elsewhere in this volume.

George Knox inherited Prehen estate, with its fine house, the woods and 3600 acres of good land when he was just thirteen, in 1845. A few years later he took up studies at Oxford, where he graduated in Law. By all accounts he was a great socialiser and it seems he continued his party-going when he returned to the Derry. He also involved himself in many aspects of the day-to-day life of the city, including the judiciary and the local militia, in which he eventually reached the rank of colonel.

But his life was destined to change. From what we have learned, it seems that George Knox, now in his early twenties, began to feel that his local duties were becoming rather restricting: the parties were beginning to lose their shine and, more to the point, were becoming too expensive. His solution was quick and effective. Quite simply he vanished from Prehen. One day he was there; the next he was gone, leaving no forwarding address. George Knox had taken off on a voyage to the ends of the earth, leaving his mother to run the Prehen estate

His friends and associates were bewildered by Colonel Knox's sudden departure and there appeared to be no way of getting in touch with him. Many years afterwards he revealed that he took great steps to conceal his whereabouts from people back in Derry. He cared not a jot that for all intents and purposes he had vanished from the face of the earth. But where did he get to? We know from reports in the press after his death that George Knox had travelled around the world, often residing for lengthy periods in some of the countries he visited. This information apart, the whole episode remained a mystery until the present day, when further details were uncovered in papers in Prehen House. Gradually the jigsaw of Colonel's Knox's missing years is coming together, piece by piece.

It seems that Knox planned an outward journey that would first take him to the far side of the globe. We know with reasonable certainty that he visited Australia, New Zealand, the Southern Pacific Ocean and countries bordering the China Seas. After this we find him in India, which was under the control of Britain at the time, and from the subcontinent we can trace him to Africa in the mid-1850s. We then find him in Algeria, so it would be reasonable to assume that he travelled across North Africa, including Egypt. Next we move on to Europe, where we locate him at Neuchâtel in Switzerland and discover that he has married a Swiss girl, Rose Grimm. The date is 1856 and he has fallen head-over-heels in love in his mid-twenties. This marriage will last for more than four decades.

By the 1860s, George Knox was growing weary of travelling and, after years of wandering, he decided it was time to return to Derry. Now picture this. It is a day in late summer and a carriage followed by a lumbering horse-drawn wagon winds its way up the long avenue to Prehen House. Out steps none other than the weather-beaten George Knox, followed, so the family annals say, by three women. Actually it was one woman and two young girls – to be precise Rose (Grimm) Knox and the couple's two daughters Virgine and Augusta. The news spread through Derry like wildfire: disbelief would be a better description. The intrepid George Knox, the Vanishing Colonel, had returned to the fold just as suddenly as he had disappeared.

And what of the lumbering wagon that pulled up outside the door of Prehen House? Gossip told of weird and wonderful things. And indeed the contents were astonishing, filled as the wagon was all the bits and pieces the Derry traveller had accumulated over his years of wandering. George Knox could not resist relics of other countries and, it seemed, the odder these were the better. His collection was described as being the envy of every museum in Ireland. There was an assortment of shields and spears and ornamental daggers from the South Pacific, sepoy drums from India, ancient duelling pistols, masks, headgear, tribal dresses from Africa, souvenirs of Napoleon III and, believe it or not, a crocodile's head. But there was something else – something that shocked George Knox's friends when they came to call – his collection of Maori warrior heads. These were the shrunken tattooed heads of Maori warriors sometimes referred to as 'moko'. They look gruesome and often seem to have an unusual, spooky presence. George Knox obtained the warrior heads in New Zealand and put them into glass jars. It seems in the beginning he had a shelf full of them, although records say that in the end only one sat upon the mantelpiece in his study at Prehen.

It was, of course, a Derry talking point and, while many visitors to Prehen House were horrified, others were curious, for the collecting of these tribal heads and animal heads had become a fad throughout Europe by the mid-1800s. Colonel George Knox, an accomplished raconteur, made light of it all, preferring to recount his great adventures. Then in time he took up his duties in the city again. He became the longest-serving member of the Workhouse Guardians, a member of the Derry Asylum Board and a Deputy-Lieutenant for Derry and Donegal. He also took a leading role in the administration of law and order and rejoined the Derry Militia. Each Sunday morning the Knoxes would set out for Glendermott Church on their pony and trap – a three-mile journey. Colonel Knox was tall and took the outside end of the pew so he could stretch his legs into the aisle. It was said that often during the minister's sermon he would leave the church and could be found outside cleaning the brasses on the pony and trap.

There was still one special city George Knox wanted to see: Paris. In the spring of 1871 Paris was just recovering from the devastating consequences of a four-month siege by Prussia. Knox set out from Derry and found the city in ruins, a scene of destruction and starvation. Nonetheless he was able to obtain keepsakes of the Paris siege and these joined his ever-growing collection of mementoes in Prehen.

After his return from Paris, George Knox took up his civic duties in Derry once more but his travelling was by no means over. He could never stay still and soon he was making regular visits to Germany, where his two young daughters had become favourites at the court of the emperor – Kaiser Wilhelm I. Years later he would spend part of every year in Europe, especially at the ancient city of Weimar in Germany. His daughter, Virgine, had married Professor Ludwig von Scheffler, an expert in the art of the Renaissance, and lived in the city. George Knox loved nothing better than to wander through the beautiful old streets of Weimar. Today it is one of Europe's great cultural sites and in past times was home to personalities such as Bach, Liszt, Schiller, Goethe and Nietzsche, the 'God is dead' philosopher. As it happened Nietzsche, who died of syphilis, was a close friend of von Scheffler and lived in the same street as the family. (Incidentally, the library in Weimar, said to be one of the finest and oldest in existence, lost many priceless volumes in a fire in 2004.)

In time the von Schefflers visited Prehen and came to play a leading role in the Knox story, especially their son George, who became the Colonel's favourite grandchild. As a boy, George was a page to Grand Duke Carl Alexander of Saxe-Weimar and was later attached to the court of the Kaiser. It was in this role that the young von Scheffler got to know all the crown heads of Europe before the First World War.

As for Colonel George Knox, he lost his beloved wife Rose in 1904. A light had gone out of his life and with it went his genial ways and great storytelling. He continued to rise at six each morning to do his paperwork, reading without glasses even at the age of seventy-eight. Reports indicate that he did not like to be disturbed and had become rather ill-tempered. In the evenings, even though he had a roaring fire in his study, he would ask his servants to pile books high around his chair to keep out the draughts.

A letter that can be seen at Prehen House indicates that George Knox knew his end was approaching. He used a bedroom at the south side of the dwelling, overlooking the River Foyle, and writing to his daughter, Virgine, in Weimar late in the summer of 1910, he notes sadly, 'My dear, you will know to come home when you hear that I have moved to your mother's old room...' He had been feeling unwell and did indeed move to this room in the autumn of the same year. It was the beginning of the end. Colonel George Knox, the Derryman with the insatiable wanderlust – 'the Vanishing Colonel' – passed away on the evening of Sunday, 22 November 1910.

from Lord Macaulay: *Life and Letters*

Saturday 1 September 1849

As soon as I had breakfasted, Sir R. Ferguson came, and walked round the walls with me. Thereafter he took me to the reading- room where I met Captain Leach and a Mr Gilmour. They too walked round the walls with me, which I have thus now gone over four times. The bastions are planted as gardens. The old pieces of ordnance lie among the flowers and the shrubs: strange antique guns of the time of Elizabeth and Charles the First. Later, Captain Leach and I crossed the wooden bridge to Waterside and took a view of the city from that quarter.

Sir Robert Ferguson was the long-serving MP for Londonderry (1830–1860). Captain Leach, who impressed Macaulay greatly, was an outstanding member of the Irish Ordnance Survey from 1844. He loved Derry, bought a house by the River Foyle and thereafter played an active role in the life of the city. The reading–room (and library) where Macaulay met Leach and Gilmore was at No. 2 Castle Street and was later the recruiting room for the First World War.

COLBY'S MOUNTAIN MEN

How Derry Changed the Map

When County Derry was selected as the 'base' for the Irish Ordnance Survey in the early 1800s it was an extraordinary stroke of good fortune. The city itself soon had an Ordnance Survey office and as a result we have a claim to fame in the history of map-making and also in the recording of local folklore. The skills learned here were to reach as far as Mount Everest during the survey of India and, as if this wasn't enough, the whole episode inspired an outstanding play well over a century later. Much of it was down to the genius of Thomas Colby and his team of brilliant assistants. Colby's 'mountain men' scaled peaks, crossed bogs and waded through rivers to create a masterwork that has since become known as Ireland's own *Doomsday Book*. At the time it was described as the best mapping in the world.

It all began in the summer of 1824, when out of the blue, a cavalcade of wagons, horses, equipment and dozens of soldiers lumbered across the old wooden bridge from Waterside into Derry. Unknown to most local people the government wanted a new land-valuation in Ireland for tax purposes and what they were witnessing was the advance survey party arriving in town. At the head of this strange entourage, suitably attired in his brilliant red military tunic, was Colonel Thomas Colby of the Royal Engineers. Colby had already made a name for himself with the Ordnance Survey in England and was the automatic choice to supervise the mapping of Ireland from top to bottom.

But why did Derry figure in such a gigantic task? The

answer lies on the nearby shoreline of the River Foyle at Magilligan. Here the land is flat as far as the eye can see and Colby felt it was the ideal spot for the 'base measurement', the starting-point for the whole process, which used a system of calculation called triangulation. Surveying requires clear sightings between points and it was anticipated that mist and haze, weather conditions that were common in Ireland, would create difficulties. These were overcome by the use of special lights and in an early test the top of Divis Mountain near Belfast was viewed from Slieve Snaght in Donegal, a distance of almost seventy miles. After much discussion it was decided that six inches to the mile would be necessary to provide the detailed mapping required. It was work that involved mathematics, statistics, scientific measurements, instrument-making and engraving as well as surveying.

For all this Colby chose some of the best brains of the time. Larcom, Portlock, Drummond, Ligar, Reid and Leach are just some of the names that occupy a proud place in the annals of Ordnance Survey. Operations commenced in Magilligan in 1827. Here giant theodolites were mounted on specially-built base towers. With these Colby got an exact line-of-sight distance of eight miles for triangulation purposes and, having achieved this, he set the survey of Ireland in motion. In all it took more than two decades to complete. Every inch of the countryside, including roads, byways, rivers, valleys and landmarks, was recorded. Peak after peak was climbed and often the soldiers had to haul theodolites weighing more than half a ton to the mountain tops.

Once the information was gathered it was sorted locally and then dispatched to Ordnance Survey headquarters in the Phoenix Park in Dublin, where an enormous volume of paper had begun to build up. In the end this staggering accumulation of facts and figures created quite a controversy because much of it lay untouched. However, when the maps and drawings produced by the engravers were published in the 1830s, they were regarded as breathtaking. This was in no small way due to Colby himself. He was a stickler for accuracy and one of his legacies was the compensation bar – a device that provided an exact measurement regardless of temperature variation. Another development was limelight, which was attributed to Thomas Drummond. Drummond's specially constructed lamps could be seen for distances of well over sixty miles and a variation of this limelight went on to be used in theatre stages in 1837. Eventually Drummond had a disagreement with Colby and left the survey to take up a post in the government, but died in 1840.

One of the many personalities who came to consult Thomas Colby in the late 1820s was George Everest, after whom the world's highest mountain was later named. Everest took a break from surveying in India to visit Colby. He was a moody man, whose ill-humour had been exacerbated by encounters with reptiles in the swamps of India. Yet his stay in Ireland was short, for he declared that the wet and misty bogs of the country would be the death of him. He hastened back to the warm subcontinent, taking some of Colby's expert staff with him and also a set of the famous compensation bars. These later played a vital role in the survey of India, another indication of Colby's contribution to Ordnance Survey.

If the mapping of Ireland was a stroke of genius, the real masterpiece was yet to come. In 1833, Colby's assistant, Thomas Larcom, had a brilliant idea when the first maps of Derry were placed in front of him. He realised that a memoir reflecting the social life of the city would be a fitting complement to such magnificent work. Indeed he believed that every parish should have its own published memoir. As a result, three of Ireland's finest scholars – John O'Donovan, George Petrie and Eugene O'Curry – were commissioned to record every possible fragment of history, traditions, folklore, personalities and social conditions throughout the country. Each memoir would contain these facts, alongside details of geography, buildings and various statistics relating to commerce, education and religion.

Mary Ann Knox, killed by her lover,
John McNaghton.

Mrs Mussenden is remembered
by the cliff-top temple
at Downhill, County Derry.

Derry from the Waterside c. 1840s.

Frederick Hervey, Earl of Bristol and Bishop of Derry, who built the Mussenden Temple in 1783.

The Mussenden Temple on the cliff-top at Downhill, County Derry.

Derry's pride, the great Minnehaha, *captained by Robert Boggs.*

Derry from the Waterside, c. *1820s.*

James D. Ogilby,
'the vanishing lover'.

Ogilby Castle, boyhood home of James D. Ogilby.

The ruins of Boom Hall, home of the Alexanders.

*The 'disappearing colonel',
George Knox (1832-1910).*

The author at the grave of
Alexander Gilfillan at Enagh Lough.

The grand old man
of grand opera, H.B. Phillips.

St Columb's Park House, Derry, where the Lavender Lady is said to appear.

Lieutenant John Prendy, whose aircraft crashed in Ardmnore.

Derry writer Kathleen Coyle.

The heiress, Nessie Linton, who came under the spell of Bird and Dill Loughrey.

Dill Loughrey with one of her prized Scottish deerhounds.

Binnion House, home of the Loughreys in Clonmany, County Donegal.

The first, and as it turned out the only memoir to be produced was the Derry volume, *Memoir of the Parish of Templemore*. 'Colby', as it is commonly referred to, has been variously described as a work of genius or a tactical disaster. At the time it became a political hot potato: politicians thought the whole operation was too expensive, others felt that Derry was the wrong city to start with and still others felt the siege of 1689 had been ignored in the book. Amidst the arguments the project lost momentum and the mountain of paper in Phoenix Park simply grew larger and larger. Yet the *Memoir* has now achieved considerable renown and status. In these modern times local historians view the book as indispensable with regard to the history of Derry. It is a unique compilation and I am not aware of any other volume that gives such extraordinary detail of a city in a past century.

The Londonderry *Memoir* was published in 1837. In all sixteen hundred copies were printed. Two hundred copies were given free to government offices and other institutions and the rest were sold at twelve shillings and sixpence each. Today 'Colby' is a highly prized and very valuable collector's item. Last and certainly not least in the hall of fame resulting from the Irish Ordnance Survey was Brian Friel's outstanding play *Translations* (1980) – a work about language and communication, which stemmed from the efforts of the mapmakers to devise English forms of Irish placenames back in 1833.

And what of Thomas Colby himself? He was said to be over-meticulous but always led from the front, encouraging his assistants. It is believed that on one occasion he walked six hundred miles in twenty-two days. When sections of the survey came to an end he would hold giant plum-pudding parties on the mountain tops, surrounded by his men. One of the features he kept concealed and which adds to his celebrity is that he had only one hand, having lost the other in a shooting accident when he was eighteen.

Colby settled in Shipquay Street in Derry and met and

married the love of his life, local girl, Elizabeth Boyd. He stayed with the Irish Ordnance Survey for twenty-four years and finally took up the post of Director-General of the Ordnance Survey in England in 1846. He died in 1852 and the headquarters of Northern Ireland Ordnance Survey were named Colby House in tribute to him.

O'DONOVAN AND PETRIE: A BRILLIANT PARTNERSHIP

As part of the Ordnance Survey the rambles of O'Donovan and Petrie throughout the length and breadth of Ireland in search of the folklore of the townlands are legendary. From the minute the two men met they became great friends, each with a magnificent degree of scholarship that complemented the other. Apart from English, John O'Donovan had mastered Irish and Latin by the age of nine. After schooling he took an interest in ancient Irish manuscripts and this interest developed greatly after he met George Petrie, who was an accomplished artist and musician and an expert in antiquities.

The combination of O'Donovan's skill in the Irish language and Petrie's knowledge of the ancient history of Ireland made them an ideal pair for delving into the country's past. Tradition holds that their scholarship, along with that of Eugene O'Curry, another great scholar who merits mention, is unsurpassed. O'Donovan was handsome and temperamental, while Petrie was calm, witty and reflective. It was a rare combination and it worked beautifully until the momentum for the memoirs hit a political stumbling block in 1837. Much of the men's time was spent chatting to old people and personalities in the various parishes. On one occasion Petrie was introduced to Jane Ross of Limavady, and this encounter later produced the renowned tune 'The Derry Air'.

As for O'Donovan, amongst many strange meetings he came across Hugh Maguiggan of Ballynascreen – a man he described as 'the Irish Don Quixote'. Locally Maguiggan had been nicknamed 'the Chevalier' on account of his exploits. Apparently, he had ridden a mad bull to Magherafelt fair. Then he leaped across the Moyola River and, as if that wasn't enough jumped his horse over a row of cows at Tobermore. 'You were as good as Sean Crossagh that leaped the Ness Falls,' said O'Donovan jokingly. 'As good and ten times better!' quipped Maguiggan. 'Sure he was only a lazy ne'er-do-well compared to me!'

George Petrie went on to make a name for himself for his expertise in Irish folk music and his paintings were acquired by the National Gallery of Ireland. He died in 1866 at the age of seventy-six. John O'Donovan was appointed Professor of Celtic Languages at Queen's College, Belfast (now the Queen's University) and became a barrister in 1847. He died in 1861 at the age of fifty-five, father of nine children, only one of whom had offspring. It is thought that O'Donovan's work in Irish has never been matched. One of his great achievements was a full translation of *The Annals of the Four Masters* from the old Irish version originally printed in Louvain in Belgium. Ironically John O'Donovan's death was attributed to rheumatic fever brought on by his exposure to the elements during his work with Ordnance Survey Ireland.

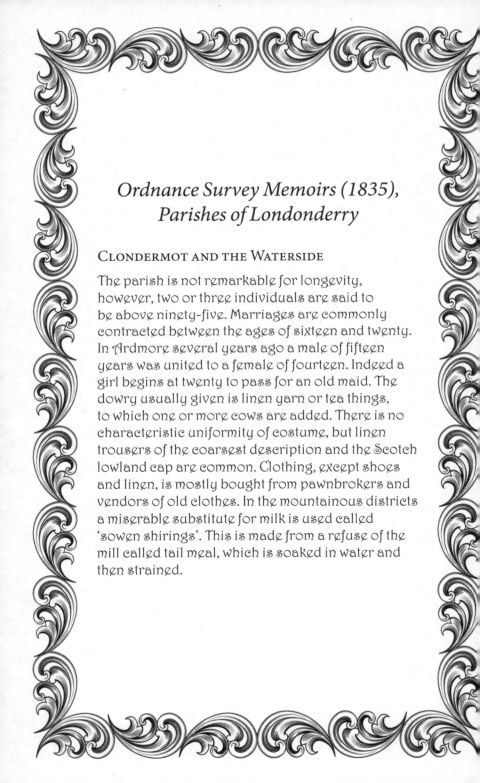

Ordnance Survey Memoirs (1835), Parishes of Londonderry

CLONDERMOT AND THE WATERSIDE

The parish is not remarkable for longevity, however, two or three individuals are said to be above ninety-five. Marriages are commonly contracted between the ages of sixteen and twenty. In Ardmore several years ago a male of fifteen years was united to a female of fourteen. Indeed a girl begins at twenty to pass for an old maid. The dowry usually given is linen yarn or tea things, to which one or more cows are added. There is no characteristic uniformity of costume, but linen trousers of the coarsest description and the Scotch lowland cap are common. Clothing, except shoes and linen, is mostly bought from pawnbrokers and vendors of old clothes. In the mountainous districts a miserable substitute for milk is used called 'sowen shirings'. This is made from a refuse of the mill called tail meal, which is soaked in water and then strained.

MYSTERIOUS WAYS

THE SECRETS OF MARY ANN KNOX AND HALF-HANGED McNAGHTEN

'If I Cannot Have Thee Then No One Else Will...'

I f ever a tale has imprinted itself indelibly in the folklore of the north-west of Ireland it must surely be the tragic love story of Mary Ann Knox of Prehen House, which is not much more than a mile outside Derry. I heard about it as a child at my mother's knee; she heard it from her father and he from his and so on – and I am sure that was the way with many local families. What is it about this yarn that has intrigued generation after generation? Perhaps it's the unresolved love story but without a doubt it must also be the behaviour of a single character, a man who has achieved legendary status, vilified by some, admired by others and universally remembered as Half-Hanged (John) McNaghten. It is hardly a sobriquet you would wish to boast about but whether he was truly villain or not I want to revisit the affair as I have been privileged to get to know Prehen House extremely well. It was here that much of the drama between McNaghten and his young love, Mary Ann Knox, was played out. Of course this all happened long ago and the challenge I have set myself is to see if any new light can be thrown on the tragedy.

Firstly, let me recall the day on which the fuse was lit in this tale of calamity and heartbreak. Picture a bleak, cold, winter's morning – 10 November 1761 – on the way from Derry to Strabane. I call it 'way' rather than 'road', for it was little more than a desolate dirt track. It was just before noon at Cloughcor, a wooded spot on an incline three miles from Strabane, when a small procession appeared, consisting of a single horse-drawn chaise followed by a large coach and four, with outriders both in front and to the rear. This little band was the Knox family of Prehen on their way to Dublin. It was a perilous journey at the best of times because of highwaymen but on this particular trip there was even more reason to be fearful. Among the party was twenty year-old Mary Ann Knox, who was being taken away from Derry to protect her from the man who claimed to be her lover – the vengeful and relentless John McNaghten.

This part of the route at Cloughcor was dangerous, as the slope slowed the carriage and, sure enough, McNaghten was lying in wait with his accomplices in a small cabin at the side of the track. He had picked his spot well and what was about to unfold was a deed so wicked that it will live forever in Irish folklore. But at this point I want to take you back to the beginning of the tale and the facts I uncovered as I delved into the Knox family archives in Prehen House.

As noted in an earlier story in this book, the word 'Prehen' comes from the Irish and means 'Place of crows'. In past times the crows could roost here with pride for local tradition holds that the ancient woods of Prehen contained the last of the great oaks of Columcille's Derry. The house itself was built around 1740 by Andrew Knox, MP for Donegal, on a bank overlooking the River Foyle. He had become the lord of the manor on his marriage to the heiress, Honoria Tomkins, who brought to the union an estate of 3600 acres. On their wedding day in 1738, Grandmother Tomkins presented Honoria with a King James family bible (published in 1709). This bible holds pride of place in Prehen House library and records that the marriage produced three children – a girl, Mary Ann, a boy, George, and an infant who died. Honoria herself entered Mary Ann's birth in the bible as 2 November 1741.

The Knox dwelling was designed by Derry architect Michael Priestley and is Georgian in style with a plain, neat, stone façade. The sandstone relief work of Scottish architect, James Gibbs, is evident in the surrounds of the doors and windows and gives the dwelling a rather quaint, old-world appearance. By the middle of the 1900s the dwelling had fallen into disrepair but in 1972 Carola and Julian Peck, in-laws of the Knoxes, came to Prehen and began to restore the house to its original Georgian splendour. It is by far the oldest residence in Derry and has that pleasant lived-in feeling of generations past in the fabric of every nook and cranny. I have been fortunate to be able to wander about the rooms where Mary Ann Knox and John McNaghten got to know one another, played hide and seek and shared their little secrets – for, as we shall see, secrets there were. Sitting in the library or in the beautiful upstairs salon of an evening I often strain my ears for spooky sounds for it's said you can sometimes hear the conversations and youthful giggles of the lovers drifting in the air. What could they tell us, I wonder? What were their secrets?

The story recalled around the firesides of the north-west saw John McNaghten as a nasty piece of work. He took advantage of the impressionable Mary Ann against the wishes of the Knoxes, killed her in a botched abduction and finished on the gallows. The seeds of all of this were sown long before. In early life McNaghten was educated at the Royal School, Raphoe, and had been involved in several youthful affrays before progressing to Trinity College in Dublin. Here he got a degree but after coming of age and inheriting the Benvarden estate in County Antrim he started to gamble heavily.

McNaghten rapidly squandered a fortune, got massively into debt and saw his pregnant young wife die after a debtors' quarrel outside their Dublin home. All in all he was what came to be known in Ireland as a 'squireen' – an outrageous young buck doing as he pleased: in plain language, a rake. But John McNaghten was no ordinary rake. He was blonde, blue-eyed and very good-looking and he had a soft manner that could charm the birds from the trees. Quite simply, men liked his jovial company and women found him irresistible. However, debts in Dublin caused him to move back to the north-west of Ireland where, with the help of loans from relatives and friends, he was able to resume his gambling.

So what of the love affair with Mary Ann Knox? The story goes that John McNaghten called upon Andrew Knox at Prehen House one summer evening after a disastrous session at the gaming table in Derry. The year was 1756 and he was thirty-two years-old. His idea was a bed for the night but Knox, a family friend, gave him an open invitation to visit at any time. McNaghten took advantage of the offer and quickly became a close friend of fifteen-year-old Mary Ann, the only daughter of the family. A portrait at Prehen shows her to be a stylish, almost coquettish young woman, with cupid's bow lips and captivating eyes that give her an impish, come-hither look. John McNaghten cut a dashing figure and there is no doubt that the girl was moonstruck. Soon they were inseparable. Her father, secure in the notion that his daughter would soon find a gentleman with a great estate, turned a blind eye on the liaison. Mama Knox, on the other hand, was heard to say that she would not mind a man like young Mister McNaghten for a son-in-law. Obviously, John McNaghten was behaving impeccably, at least while at Prehen. But storm clouds were gathering, for the talk about Derry was that he had squandered his Benvarden estate on the turn of a card.

Now comes a major issue in this sinister tale: did McNaghten, now in crippling debt, deliberately ingratiate himself with Mary Ann to take advantage of her dowry of £6000? He was accused of this afterwards but never admitted it. What is known is that the pair certainly talked about the possibility of marrying but Andrew Knox told McNaghten privately that he would not countenance any nuptials. However, John told Mary Ann that her father did agree to their union but that not a word should be uttered for the time being. On the strength of his assurances, the gullible girl agreed to go through with a marriage ceremony. Some say it was simply a mock affair but I discovered that John and Mary met in secret at 20 Shipquay Street in Derry, the home of Joshua Swetenham, with a young witness called Hamilton. It does appear that they were officially married, as the announcement appeared in a directory of the time.

After this, McNaghten began to declare openly that Mary Ann was his wife and Andrew Knox countered this by having the marriage declared void in court. Battle lines were drawn. McNaghten, now banished from Prehen, was in a fighting mood, insisting that Mary Ann was his, while the Knoxes and their friends were equally intent on keeping her away from him. It was a stand-off, which served only to infuriate McNaghten all the more.

So what was the real position with Mary Ann and John? By this time the girl was in her late teens, so one would assume that she knew what she was doing. The question is – was it naivety, or was it love at any cost, that ruled her emotions? The strange thing about the tale is that we never really know what the girl was thinking. We can assume that she was captivated by John. That she later rebuffed him in the garden of a friend of the Knoxes may simply have been her way of saying that it was neither the time nor the place. As for McNaghten, why did he continue to claim her when he was so aware of the father's objections? Was it true love or was it her dowry that attracted him? Reports indicate that he became more aggressive by the minute, his mood menacing, if not irrational. He would not take no for an answer, regardless of the wishes of the Knoxes. And it was this belligerence of McNaghten that eventually prompted the family to remove the girl to Dublin.

Before we return to that anxious little band of Knoxes weaving its way up the slope at Cloughcor, let us pause to look for a moment at the days just before the party set off. Here we uncover a puzzling, even alarming aspect of what was soon to occur and it may indicate just how close Mary Ann and John were. Earlier I mentioned secrets, so apart from the secret marriage and the usual little intimacies of lovers, what might these have been? Firstly, records at Prehen reveal that the affair between the pair had been going on for more than three years so they must have known and understood each other very well and perhaps made plans. Secondly, it has been discovered that after McNaghten was banished from Prehen the young lovers kept in contact with each other by means of notes left at what was known as the 'post office tree'. Servants ferried these secret messages back and forth so there was obviously some sympathy for the match inside Prehen House itself. This raises an absolutely crucial question: did the servants get word to McNaghten about the family trip to Dublin? Furthermore, was Mary Ann party to this message and did McNaghten reply that he would rescue her? If so, there arises an almost unthinkable hypothesis: that Mary Ann may have known something about John's plans to spirit her away, while perhaps not being fully aware of the details.

This is, of course, conjecture but, while investigating the Cloughcor ambush, I uncovered an odd little story amongst the Prehen archives. One of the Knox party was a young family servant David McCullagh, who later became a blacksmith. Upon retirement he lived in a little cottage on the Prehen estate and remarkably had passed into his hundredth year when, one day, ten-year-old George Knox, the last of the Knoxes (who died in 1910 and is mentioned elsewhere in this book) came upon his cottage. There in the course of an afternoon McCullagh recalled vividly the circumstances surrounding the death of Mary Ann for the wide-eyed boy – an account that has contributed greatly to our knowledge of the tragedy.

Back now to Cloughcor on that cold November morning in 1761 and a scene of utter mayhem as McNaghten and his men ambushed the Knox coach. Bloodshed was inevitable: McNaghten must surely have realised this beforehand. It is thought that Mary Ann was mortally wounded attempting to shield her father when McNaghten fired into the coach. One story goes that he deliberately shot Mary Ann saying – 'If I cannot have thee then no one else will...' Later, at his trial in Lifford, he declared how much he loved her and as if to prove this he climbed the gallows a second time after the rope broke initially. Custom would have allowed him to walk free and the crowd was sympathetic. Instead, with his enigmatic death he caused the story of Mary Ann to live for posterity and endowed himself with one of the most loathsome names you could ever imagine – Half-Hanged McNaghten.

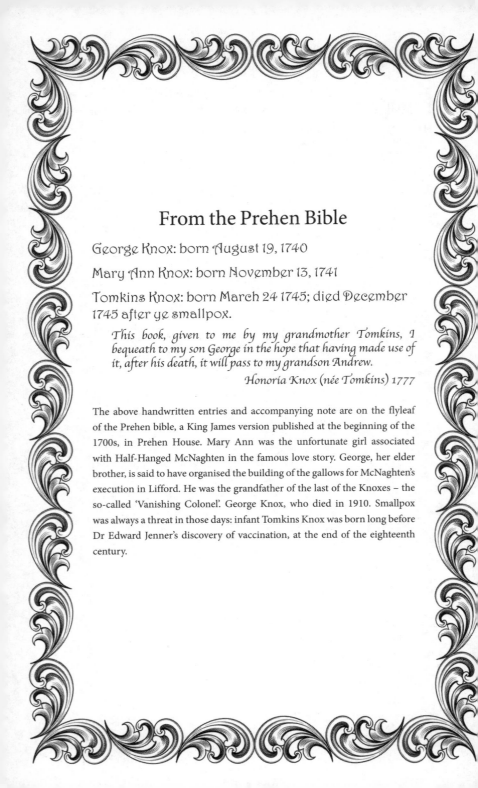

From the Prehen Bible

George Knox: born August 19, 1740

Mary Ann Knox: born November 13, 1741

Tomkins Knox: born March 24 1745; died December 1745 after ye smallpox.

> *This book, given to me by my grandmother Tomkins, I bequeath to my son George in the hope that having made use of it, after his death, it will pass to my grandson Andrew.*
>
> *Honoria Knox (née Tomkins) 1777*

The above handwritten entries and accompanying note are on the flyleaf of the Prehen bible, a King James version published at the beginning of the 1700s, in Prehen House. Mary Ann was the unfortunate girl associated with Half-Hanged McNaghten in the famous love story. George, her elder brother, is said to have organised the building of the gallows for McNaghten's execution in Lifford. He was the grandfather of the last of the Knoxes – the so-called 'Vanishing Colonel'. George Knox, who died in 1910. Smallpox was always a threat in those days: infant Tomkins Knox was born long before Dr Edward Jenner's discovery of vaccination, at the end of the eighteenth century.

Derry's Moving Statue

*...A Sinister Lost Diamond
and a Long-Suffering Donegal Wife*

John Lawrence was educated in Derry and as Viceroy of India in 1863 became monarch of the subcontinent in all but name. Hailed as a saviour, he brought peace to a troubled country and was an outstanding reformer and administrator. Yet he somehow managed to mislay one of the world's most precious diamonds. Some would argue, however, that at least he had the good sense to come back home in search of a wife. These days Lawrence is all but forgotten but he has left one other strange legacy, his statue. At present located at Foyle and Londonderry College, it appears to like travelling. Not that it materialises in odd places or anything like that but the ten-foot-high bronze sculpture of John Lawrence has been across the world and back and even here in Derry it wants to keep on moving.

Many years ago I travelled to Ballinspittle in County Cork in search of the famous moving statue there. People said it rocked back and forth, although I must say that I saw nothing. But little did I think at the time that here in Derry we had a moving variety of our own – one with a fondness for travel.

If you met John Lawrence wandering the streets of Derry in the early 1800s you probably wouldn't have given him a second glance. Descriptions of him vary from plain to uninspiring; most likely he was quiet and unpretentious. Certainly there was nothing to indicate that here was a future Viceroy of India. John Lawrence's father was Colonel Alexander Lawrence from

County Derry and his mother, Letitia Knox, was from County Donegal. There were twelve children in all in the family and four of the sons, including John and his brother Henry, were pupils at Foyle College. It's likely that the boys saw little of their parents in those early days. Colonel Lawrence spent most of his active life in India and Ceylon. It was usual for children to be educated back home and the prestigious Foyle College in Derry was a natural choice for a family that was always proud of its Irish roots.

Henry Lawrence, John's elder brother, was at Foyle before him and eventually went into the army in India. In time, John left Foyle and went to the East India Company College (later Haileybury College), where civil servants were trained for India. It was a reluctant move as John too wanted to join the army but the family benefactor said no. As a result John arrived in Calcutta at the age of seventeen to start his extraordinary career in what was generally referred to as the ICS (Indian Civil Service). He rose rapidly through the ranks. In today's world we'd call him a workaholic: never stopping, never taking any leave, he was a dedicated administrator, who stuck rigidly to the book. However, on the way up he disagreed with his brother Henry over the administration of the Punjab, a row that eventually led to Henry being relieved of his post Thereafter, the relationship between the two brothers was a bitter one, to say the least.

Lawrence was eventually made Viceroy of India in 1863. In effect he was the country's ruler and was given the title Lord Lawrence of the Punjab. One of his tasks was to subdue India's North-West Frontier. He would have been familiar with places that we now hear about on the news: the Khyber Pass, Kandahar, Kabul and the magnificent Peshawar. Here he diced with the notorious chieftain Dost Mohamed in circumstances very similar to those we see in Afghanistan today.

Work kept Lawrence from marrying but when he felt it was time to wed he couldn't find a woman to please him. 'Searching for a wife is just a proper calamity,' he was heard to say. Eventually, he came back to Donegal, where he met a clergyman's daughter, Harriet Hamilton, and at last he tied the knot. We can only guess that Harriet was a long-suffering woman, for with Lawrence's gruff ways and his refusal even to take a holiday she must have had the patience of Job.

But how did Lawrence become a moving statue? Well, I dare say you have to be pretty famous to have your statue cast in bronze and it is astonishing that no fewer than three were made of John Lawrence. Two of these were placed in London squares in the latter part of the 1800s, while a third went to Calcutta. Then, in 1887, one of the London statues was sent out to Lahore in India. This part of the world would eventually become Pakistan and, significantly for our story, this was the start of the moving statue saga.

We travel forward seventy-six years now to a bitter March day in Derry in 1963. At the former Foyle College premises on the aptly named Lawrence Hill, a crowd of governors, old boys, staff and pupils, were gathered round a draped object sitting on a plinth. At a given signal and to loud applause the covering was removed to reveal none other than Lord Lawrence – or, at least his bronze statue – indeed, the very statue that had travelled out to Lahore all those decades earlier.

How did it all come about? Herein lies another tale. Firstly, the statue was a victim of the Troubles of the late 1940s, which came after independence and led to the creation of Pakistan. Then in the early 1960s, of all the indignities, a Foyle old boy heard that it was lying upended on a scrap-heap in Lahore. By all accounts it was a rather sorry sight, having lost its right hand and a sword held in the left hand. Undaunted, the Foyle Old Boys' Association decided that Lawrence should come back to his former school, so they launched a campaign to bring him home. Help was on hand: the P&O Shipping Company volunteered to bring the statue from Karachi back to London. Mind you, even to get to Karachi meant a journey of several hundred miles from Lahore, in the north of Pakistan. But in spite of all the difficulties Lawrence was on the move again and eventually arrived in London.

The story was far from over, for the statue still had to get to Derry by rail and ferry and that was only after a visit to a London foundry, where it got a new right hand and sword. Even at that, Lawrence Hill in Derry wasn't to be the statue's last resting place. Five years later Foyle relocated to a new school in the Springtown district and, naturally enough, Lord Lawrence went too. I had a look at him recently and apart from weathering he seems in fine fettle. Up to now he has moved half-a-dozen times and travelled almost 10,000 miles.

When one considers this particular statue of Lawrence, it comes as no surprise that it has drawn much comment over the years. Its subject comes across as rather cavalier-like and portly – a swaggering sort of man, strangely attired in an ordinary three-quarter-length coat and with what looks like a casual shirt. Then there is the odd combination of a pen in one hand and a sword in the other. It is believed that Boehm, the famous sculptor who made the statue, wanted to convey Lawrence's nature, hence the workaday clothes, the pen and the sword bearing precisely the message that the pen is mightier than the sword. Apparently, this was always the way John Lawrence did business. However some people argued that the sword had more than a symbolic purpose; Lawrence would not hesitate to use force if need be.

One thing we do know about Lawrence is that he was very absent-minded. The story goes that he was given the magnificent Koh-i-Noor diamond for safe-keeping while in the Punjab in 1849. This white stone – known as the 'mountain of light'– was one of the largest jewels in the world. It was reckoned to be more than 5000 years old and a history of mystery, murder, mayhem and ill-luck was inextricably linked to it. Although the Koh-i-Noor was known to be priceless, Lawrence casually put it in his waistcoat pocket and thought nothing more about it. Some time later he was asked to return the diamond but, amazingly, had forgotten where he'd put it. A search revealed nothing and it was only when a servant said he'd found 'an old piece of glass' that the Koh-i-Noor was recovered. It is now part of the British Crown Jewels, under lock and key in the Tower of London.

Weird and wonderful are the twists and turns of fate. Lying at rest in Carrigans graveyard, just six miles from Lawrence's statue, is Lady Walker, who is associated with another mislaid precious stone in India, the Jacob Diamond. Said to shine with a brilliant blue light, it is the size of an egg. Lady Walker, who came to live in Donegal, spent much of her life in India and in the early 1900s she became a personal friend of the richest man on earth, the Nizam of Hyderabad. The Nizam, whose son had a different Rolls Royce for every day of the week, bought the Jacob Diamond on an impulse.

Lady Walker would often have been able to admire it for, true to form, the Nizam had it on his desk where it served as a makeshift paper-weight. In time he got bored with the gem and hid it away for safety. The trouble was he then died suddenly and it seemed that the famous diamond would be lost for ever. Odd to relate, years later, it was discovered in the toe of one of the Nizam's slippers. He owned a thousand pairs and they had all been laid side by side in his two-hundred-and-seventy-foot long wardrobe. The Jacob Diamond is now owned by the Indian government. Like the Koh-i-Noor it is priceless and regarded as a national treasure.

Finally, dare we ask if Derry's moving statue will ever budge again? Of course it will. When Foyle and Londonderry College relocates to the Waterside, I wouldn't mind betting who'll be first on the low loader – Lord Lawrence of course!

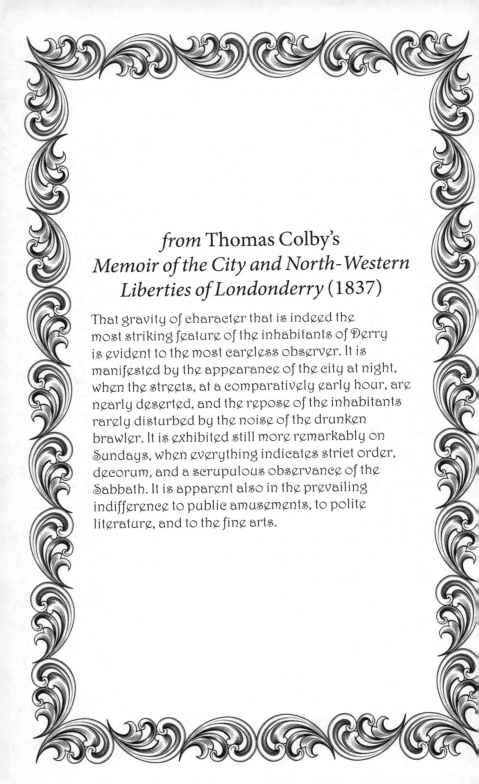

from Thomas Colby's
Memoir of the City and North-Western Liberties of Londonderry (1837)

That gravity of character that is indeed the most striking feature of the inhabitants of Derry is evident to the most careless observer. It is manifested by the appearance of the city at night, when the streets, at a comparatively early hour, are nearly deserted, and the repose of the inhabitants rarely disturbed by the noise of the drunken brawler. It is exhibited still more remarkably on Sundays, when everything indicates strict order, decorum, and a scrupulous observance of the Sabbath. It is apparent also in the prevailing indifference to public amusements, to polite literature, and to the fine arts.

THE LAST DUEL

A Strange Twist of Fate on the Shores of Lough Swilly

The last duel fought in Ireland took place just a few miles from Derry, near the town of Buncrana, on Lough Swilly. It turned out to be a weird affair and came to light only through the recollections of an old man just before he died. He revealed a secret he had harboured for over sixty years and it turned out to be a tale with the strangest twist you could ever imagine. Looking at the beauty of Lough Swilly these days, it's hard to believe it was often the scene of great violence in times past. So perhaps the odd duel or two may be regarded as little out of the ordinary. Yet the encounter at Buncrana in 1810 does catch the imagination; not only was it played out in the most bizarre fashion but it went down in history as the last duel to take place in Ireland.

William Todd, the man at the centre of the story, lived in Buncrana Castle in the early 1800s. The castle stands to this day and you can reach it by crossing the beautiful eighteenth-century bridge spanning the Crana River just where it enters Lough Swilly. Colonel George Vaughan built this castle in 1718. In truth it is really an elegant house and bears no resemblance whatsoever to any sort of fortification. It was so named because it replaced the existing O'Doherty stronghold, the only evidence of which is the square, medieval tower known as the Keep, which was probably a Norman castle in earlier times.

The colourful Sir Cahir O'Doherty, the Irish youth brought up as an English gentleman, who later led a rebellion against the Crown, would have been a visitor here in the early 1600s.

The Keep was eventually burned by English troops. You can still find traces of similar O'Doherty strongholds on the Swilly at Inch, Burt and Aileach. No doubt Vaughan thought the warring was over and felt the time was right to build a gentleman's seat near Buncrana. It's interesting to note that this site, consisting of the castle and the Keep, was originally *Bun Cranncha* ('Foot of the Crana') and that Vaughan established the town in its present position when his new residence was completed. Incidentally, descendants of Vaughan, the Reverend George Vaughan Sampson and his brother William, were to leave their marks on our local history. George was a teacher and author of the famous *Statistical Survey of Derry*, while William joined the United Irishmen and later became a brilliant barrister.

When William Todd acquired Buncrana Castle from the Vaughans in the early 1800s, Ireland was just about cooling down after the Rebellion of 1798 so I'm sure he hoped for some peaceful days. But it wasn't to be. It appears that he got into a dispute with a man called Hartley (some believed the name was Bateman) and that this eventually led to a confrontation between the pair.

Details of what happened were eventually swallowed by the mists of time and we would know nothing about the feud had it not been for the eighty-year-old George White, who was Todd's manservant at the time. Before he died in 1881, he revealed details of the incident. White recalled the worsening of relations between Todd and Hartley back in that first decade of the century. Then came the challenge. It appears that Todd had no experience with firearms and may have had little appetite for a duel. However, he asked White to be his second and at first light they set off from Buncrana Castle to meet Hartley at the chosen location. This was a remote spot near Druminderry Bridge, just a little beyond the town. En route Todd's horse lost a shoe and this caused them to approach the bridge by a different route – an occurrence that was to have a dramatic influence on that fateful day. As the sun came up

White loaded a pair of pistols and Todd gave Hartley his choice of weapon.

At this juncture a brief look at the history of duelling will help us to understand what unfolded at Druminderry Bridge all those years ago. Firstly, duelling was the ancient way of defending a man's honour; only gentlemen could take part. During the 1700s pistols replaced swords. When an affront occurred the offended party would throw a glove on the ground before his enemy. This action came about from medieval knights' practice of 'throwing down the gauntlet'. The slap on the face with a glove often portrayed in the movies was a later addition. Duels took place in remote areas at early light to avoid attention and the number of paces between the parties and the sequence of firing were agreed beforehand by the seconds or assistants. All sides had to obey what was known as the Code Duello. Ireland had its own code, which forbade men shooting to miss.

Back now to Druminderry Bridge, where Hartley, who was known to be a good shot, fired and missed. In reply, Todd shot low and wide, but fate was waiting in the wings, for the bullet ricocheted off a rock and Hartley received a fatal wound. Naturally enough the affair was the talk of the land, especially when Todd was brought to trial. In the end he was found guilty of Hartley's death and sentenced to be branded – the penalty at the time. However, such was the sympathy for Todd that the branding iron was not heated. Thus, despite being 'cold branded', he walked away with his honour intact. Afterwards, several attempts were made on Todd's life by Hartley's sister but in the end the two families were reconciled. William Todd died in 1813 and his manservant, George White, revealed one further startling fact. By taking a different route to Druminderry Bridge on the day of the duel because of the lost horseshoe Todd most certainly avoided death, as an assassin was lying in wait for him.

Wolfe Tone, one of the leaders of the United Irishman, was held in Buncrana Castle when the French vessel *Hoche* was captured in Lough Swilly in the autumn of 1798. The spot where he disembarked on the shore is quite close by. It is believed that it was a friend from his student days who identified Wolfe Tone. Then on 3 November he was taken to Derry jail before being transported to Dublin. Fifteen years earlier Tone himself was nearly involved in a duelling incident with Ireland's greatest dueller, Richard Martin ('Humanity Dick'). Martin had more than a hundred duels to his credit but refused to challenge Tone, who was having an affair with his wife. In return Martin got £10,000 compensation, which he donated to charity. Tone's ship was later renamed HMS *Donegal* and served in the war against Spain before being broken up in 1845.

Odd to relate, sixteen years after the Buncrana dispute Scotland's last duel took place and had many similarities to the affair on the Lough Swilly. In the year 1826 David Landale, a linen merchant of Kirkcaldy, was forced into a duel with his local bank manager, George Morgan, after arguments about a loan. Morgan was highly skilled in shooting, while Landale had no experience whatsoever. Indeed he was so upset he became ill. Attempts by the seconds of both men to bring about a peaceful resolution came to nothing and Landale was obliged to purchase a set of duelling pistols.

Convinced that he would not survive, David Landale sat up all night before the duel writing his will and praying. Morgan on the other hand, turned up, cool and collected, at the appointed hour, believing he would be the victor. But his shot missed. Then Landale, eyes practically shut, took aim and, amazingly, shot Morgan through the heart. In the ensuing trial, public sympathy was with Landale. The jury found him not guilty and he walked away a free man. Nineteen years later the last recorded duel in England took place, in 1845.

BURKE AND HARE

'We Might as Well Be Hung for a Sheep as a Lamb...'

The names Burke and Hare conjure up terror – and rightly so. They were the first well-known serial killers of modern times and even today the residue of their atrocious deeds lingers on in the dark, winding alleyways of Edinburgh. To hear that these depraved killers had links with the north-west is unnerving to say the least – but is there any substance to the story? In order to find out I've been combing the local archives for evidence of the evil pair and I've travelled to Edinburgh to see what further facts might be uncovered.

I never pass old Glendermott graveyard in Derry's Waterside without thinking about the infamous Burke and Hare and I can tell you it sends a shiver down my spine. Glendermott is an ancient burial ground and I often wonder if it was the scene of grave-robbing in early times. Thus the notion of Burke and Hare, who, by the way, were not really grave robbers in the end.

In those days grave-robbers were cynically called 'Resurrection' men. They would dig up corpses, steal the valuables, then pass the remains on to doctors for dissection. In the early years of the nineteenth century Edinburgh was a leading centre for medical training. Corpses were needed for dissection, an indispensable part of medical training, and Scottish law had severe regulations about the cadavers that might be used. Only the corpses of hanged criminals were eligible, a stricture that even in a city like Edinburgh meant there were very few specimens available. As a result grave-robbing was rife. In fact things became so bad that families had to guard the graves of their loved ones at night. Special watchtowers were built for this purpose and may still be seen at St Cuthbert's Church in Edinburgh and in Glasnevin cemetery in Dublin.

As for Burke and Hare, although they were known as body-snatchers, in fact they were killers who sold the corpses of their victims to Edinburgh's medical men. But how did the evil pair take up such a ghastly trade? Tradition holds that they had their roots right here in the north-west, in Derry and Tyrone. William Burke came from Urney, just outside Strabane in County Tyrone. He married a local girl and fathered a large family. In between times he tried several trades, before joining the Donegal Militia. Still he could not settle and eventually, in 1818, he abandoned his wife and went to work on the Union Canal in Scotland. It was about this time that he met the villainous William Hare, who ran a lodging house in Edinburgh.

It is believed that Hare came from County Derry, although some argue that his home place was Newry in County Down. What is certain is that the pair hit it off straight away. Burke was quiet and intense by nature and it appears that Hare had narrow scheming eyes and a twisted mouth that conveyed unbelievable cruelty. The murderous partnership came about by accident after an old man died in Hare's lodging house. Cheated of the rent, it dawned on the duo that they could recoup the money by bringing the old man's remains to a surgeon in the same way as grave robbers. They found a welcome at the home of Dr Robert Knox, who paid them a generous sum for the body, with no questions asked. He also indicated that he would take as many bodies as they could find. Thereafter Burke and Hare set out to get what was described as a regular supply of 'fresh' corpses. As a result they became ruthless serial killers – indeed, they have the unenviable reputation of being the first such in modern history.

What makes the flesh creep is the cold-blooded manner in which Burke and Hare carried out their awful deeds. They would befriend the victim and invite him or her to the lodging house for a drink. Then there would be a joke or two from the leering Hare as the unsuspecting man or woman was plied with alcohol until drunk. After that it was suffocation with a pillow, then delivery of the corpse as quickly as possible to Dr Knox; speed was everything.

As business boomed Hare's lodging house became the scene of debauched parties, where Edinburgh's down-and-outs found that a warm welcome awaited them. What they didn't realise was that some who entered would never leave again – at least not alive. Hare's domain was a place of rickety staircases and dark corridors. Some people later recalled the dreadful stench of death in the house and there was an abundance of straw, presumably used as a temporary hiding place for the latest victim. Another feature of the place was Hare's hideous laugh, that could often be heard echoing throughout the house.

Time went by and as the catalogue of murders mounted people began to notice that local personalities where vanishing from Edinburgh's streets. Among them were a youth known as Daft Jamie and a young prostitute called Mary Patterson. At this stage Burke and Hare were almost on friendly terms with the usually aloof Dr Knox. However, as it turned out, it was Knox's own medical students who first raised the alarm. They recognised the corpse of Mary Patterson as a girl from the neighbourhood and upon examination concluded that she had met a violent death. Burke was undeterred and despite questions from the authorities he persuaded Hare to continue. 'Sure we might as well be hung for a sheep as a lamb,' he quipped. Strangely, it's an expression that has lived on in the English language.

But they were rather prophetic words. The next murder turned out to be their last. It came about that Mary Doherty, a woman believed to have been from this part of the world, went to Edinburgh in search of her son. Plied with drink by Burke and Hare, poor Mary succumbed in the usual way to suffocation. But a friend who came looking for her found her blood-covered body concealed in a heap of straw and

informed the police. As a result, Burke, his lady friend, Helen
McDougal, and Hare and his wife were jointly accused of the
crime. But the police had little evidence and it was not until the
sly Hare turned King's evidence on Burke that the case was able
to proceed. The trial duly began on Christmas Eve 1827 and
gripped the imagination of the public for the next month.

In the end Burke was found guilty of murdering Mary
Doherty, Mary Patterson and the youth known as Daft Jamie.
In all, it was believed that there were at least thirty murders. As
for body-snatching, while Burke and Hare denied this, no one
believed them. So the notion persists to this day that they too
were body-snatchers. William Burke went to the gallows on
28 January 1828 before a crowd of 25,000. Hundreds of people
filed past the body when it was cut down and then a group of
young doctors dissected it. It was said to be one of the most
gruesome spectacles ever witnessed in Edinburgh. Meanwhile
Hare was set free, along with his wife and Helen McDougal,
Burke's partner. Shortly afterwards the two women vanished
but William Hare wandered the length and breadth of the
land in fear of his life until he was eventually blinded in a lime
kiln by fellow-workers who had discovered his true identity.
No case was found against Dr Knox but he became a much-
ridiculed figure in Edinburgh.

After my research in the Derry area my next stop was
Edinburgh. Today the legend of Burke and Hare is one of the
city's main tourist attractions. You can visit the favourite grave-
yards of the body-snatchers: St Cuthbert's, Canongate, and
Grey Friars Kirk. Of course, strictly speaking, these weren't
the hangouts of Burke and Hare but they set the scene in a
macabre way. Since I was in pursuit of the terrible pair, I spent
some time wandering around Edinburgh's atmospheric old
streets. It's not hard to imagine those dreadful times and Hare's
hideous laughter.

As I strolled along I recalled the famous rhyme that brought
much mirth in the taverns of Edinburgh after Burke's hanging:

Up the close and down the stair,
In the house with Burke and Hare.
Burke's the butcher; Hare's the thief.
Knox the man who buys the beef!

Another weird side of the affair was that during the public dissection after the hanging, the doctors removed a portion of Burke's skin. This was used to cover a pocket book which is now in the museum of the Royal College of Surgeons in Edinburgh. Burke's skeleton was also preserved and can be seen in Edinburgh University.

My last call in Edinburgh in search of Burke and Hare was Bread Street, one of their favourite haunts. These days, to put it mildly, it's a rather dingy place but apart from that, I was in for a shock. As I rounded a corner, there to my amazement I saw 'Burke and Hare'. Not, of course, the real Burke and Hare but a pub called after them. It's hard to believe that keeping the name of the dreadful duo alive in Edinburgh today is 'The World-Famous Burke and Hare Lap-dancing Club'!

The Legend of Binnion Sands

A Derry Bishop Snubbed
and a Secret Midnight Burial

Binnion Bay lies just beyond Clonmany, a mile or two from Ballyliffin in County Donegal. It's a scene of wild Irish beauty but for centuries there has been another side to this enigmatic place. Binnion has harboured tales of tyrannical landlords, sinister happenings, a ghost or two and even a mermaid thrown in for good measure. Yet in such a mysterious setting one legend stands out above all; it's a tale about a tenacious family, a sensational row with a bishop and a secret midnight burial.

On the night of Friday 23 July 1915 one of the strangest sights you are ever likely to see took place in the graveyard of St Mary's Church in Clonmany. There, in secrecy and by candlelight, a plain black coffin was lowered into the earth. It was the remains of the formidable Fr Edward Loughrey PP, a turbulent priest of the Derry diocese. He was a man who caused a sensation in his own time, a true son of one of the most resolute and legendary families ever to grace these parts – the Loughreys of Binnion House.

Just outside Clonmany and looking down across Binnion Bay, you can spot Binnion House sheltering behind a scattering of trees not far from the beach. The dwelling lies under Binnion Hill ('Little Peak'), a shoulder of grey rock that reaches out dramatically into the ocean and seems to be split in two by a great stone famine wall that wriggles its way up the hillside. The sheer isolation of the place brings thoughts of R.D.

Blackmore's famous novel, *Lorna Doone*, into one's head and, oddly enough, the townland known as Doon-ally (Dunally) is nearby. Binnion Bay is flanked to the east by Ballyliffin strand and to the west by Tullagh Bay. Familiar landmarks are Dunaff Head, Suil Rock and Glashedy Island. An ancient signpost on Clonmany Bridge near the ruin of Straid Protestant Church tells you that Derry is nineteen miles away. That's old Irish miles of course: it's nearer twenty-four in today's miles.

So what was behind the clandestine burial of Fr Loughrey in Clonmany in 1915? To unravel the mystery we have to retrace his last journey piece by piece and therein lies a weird tale. He died on Tuesday, 20 July 1915 in Dungiven, County Derry, the centre of his parish. Two days later Bishop Charles McHugh travelled out from Derry to preside over his requiem mass at the local St Patrick's Church. The bishop was in for a shock, for Fr Loughrey's remains had vanished. In fact they were on the train on their way into the Waterside station in Derry. The label on the plain black coffin read simply: 'St Mary's Chapel, Clonmany'. The coffin had no nameplate and no mountings. In a life of bold, if not brash confrontations, Fr Loughrey's last gesture was his biggest, a snub to his bishop that was well planned in every detail – even to having his favourite horse, Black Tom, draw his remains the short distance to Dungiven railway station.

It is quite possible that the late Fr Loughrey and the bishop passed each other on the way, for the train route was much used in those days. Whatever the case, the next we hear is that while the requiem mass was progressing in Dungiven, Joe Loughrey, a Derry solicitor and brother of the priest, collected the remains and brought them to St Columba's Church, Waterside. After mass the following morning Joe travelled with the coffin on a horse-drawn hearse all the way to Clonmany – a difficult, all-day journey at the time.

There was no doubting the achievements of Fr Loughrey. A man of great intellect, he had been a builder of churches and schools, a defender of people's rights, a supreme orator and a friend of all religious traditions. For many, Edward Loughrey could all but walk on water. However, his tendency to be single-minded and outspoken meant continual brushes with authority and as a result he was often at the centre of controversy. Quite simply he would not tolerate interference in anything he did and it was this side of his unyielding nature that eventually led to the unbelievable battle with Bishop McHugh.

The conflict arose over an incident regarding a pupil in Dungiven Boys' School in 1907. In the resulting dispute and with his brother Joseph's support, Fr Loughrey refused to budge in what soon became a war of attrition between himself, the National Education Board and the Bishop. In the end, getting no satisfaction from Bishop McHugh, he left him with the parting salvo: 'My Lord, I desire to respectfully inform you I go now to Rome to lay my complaints in proper hands' (those of the Pope). The drama was followed eagerly day by day in Derry and the surrounding parishes. It was the sensation of the times; a priest might disagree with his bishop but to go over his head to the Pope in an act of defiance was unheard of.

In the end Fr Loughrey's actions backfired. He lost control of his schools and I believe it shook his Loughrey pride to the foundations. His way of responding was to plan the secret removal of his remains to his birthplace at Clonmany (and of course Binnion) rather than let others, his adversaries, put the official seal on his ministry. The message was that the Loughreys would have their way in the end.

So where did such haughtiness come from? Well, perhaps it was always in the blood, but surely Binnion House and the nearby mysterious sands helped to shape the unflinching Loughrey temperament. There is a beautiful but raw wildness there, where at times you have to set your face into a bitter northerly wind whipping in from Malin Head. Young Loughreys would have been toughened by sea bathing in all weathers, wandering the shore and doing physical work on their farm. No doubt their imaginations were fired by the stories of the colourful characters and many strange happenings in these lands they were heir to.

Clonmany is a delightful but melancholy place. Tradition says that you can meet a mermaid on Binnion sands or encounter long dead souls coming and going on the lonely paths around the beach. Under Binnion Hill – so the story goes – a piper entered *Poll an Phíobaire* ('The Piper's Cave'), the cave that some say has no end. Off he went playing a special air, 'Girls will be old women before I return', and that was the last that was ever heard of him. Some people say that you can hear music coming in on the breeze when the fairies rest on Glashedy Island en route to their summer pastures; others without flinching will tell you that the pirate Connla's crock of gold is hidden somewhere inside the cliffs of Binnion.

I suppose the Binnion legend really begins in the late 1700s when Michael Loughrey, a bright and handsome lad, was adopted by an English family called Buchanan, who owned Binnion House and much of the land around Clonmany. Michael helped in his father's tavern in Moville and made such an impression on the Buchanans that they took him to live with them in England and brought him up as their son. Then, in 1814, the Buchanans transferred everything to Michael Loughrey for a nominal sum. Loughrey was a man of many hues. From what we know of him he had a very resolute nature. He was also shrewd and thoroughly Anglicised but more especially he was a devout Catholic who suddenly found himself with a vast amount of land in an area where landlordism had a bad name and Binnion was at the centre of it.

Binnion House, which Loughrey then rebuilt, had originally been the home of Colonel Daniel McNeal, a defender of Derry in the siege of 1689 and later a fighter at the Battle of the Boyne. McNeal, a tyrannical landlord, was notorious for abducting girls in the vicinity. In order to placate the local families he would allot them a rood of land. You can find what is known as a 'McNeal Rood' between Clonmany and Ballyliffin in the registers. McNeal was to perish in 1709, suffering an awful death at the hands of local men in retribution for his villainous ways. Next came the Buchanans and after them Michael Loughrey. In time his children began to grow up at Binnion. Michael's marriage produced seven boys; two died fairly young but of the others, three – John, Joe and Edward – were to add to the Loughrey legend. The latter two we have already encountered and while they were stirring up folk in Derry, John, the eldest son, was doing likewise in the area around Binnion Bay, driven on by the Loughrey flinty and steadfast nature.

In competent Loughrey style, John built the modern village of Clonmany in 1850 but proceeded to alienate his tenants with disputes that raged during the land wars of the 1870s. He met a strange fate, being gored to death by his own bull in 1901 – an event greeted with delight in Clonmany and celebrated in song throughout his own lands. Later Loughreys displayed much talent, having among them surgeons, engineers and a famous cellist. A daughter of the famous Irish sculptor, John Hogan, and his Italian wife Cornelia Bevhiari married into the family, and later still the Grant family became custodians of the estate.

The dwelling itself has the style of an Irish manor house. Warm and comfortable, it has that lived-in feeling you often get in older buildings. It is easy to imagine the strong-willed, immovable Loughreys going about their business in earlier times around this solid old residence. Even after he became a priest, Fr Loughrey came back to Binnion to work the farm. So his heart was in the place, which was always there to give him time out from those fierce Loughrey battles.

And when Fr Loughrey was no more, those battles continued. Solicitor Joe Loughrey's daughters were the famous Derry dog breeders familiarly known as Bird and Dill. Their story is told elsewhere in this volume.

By the 1970s the Loughreys had gone from Derry but the Binnion ties exist to this day, as do the many memories of this formidable family. In these lands of Clonmany one still wonders if any of the early Loughreys are among those ghosts said to haunt the local paths. And is McNeal's ghost also hereabouts? On the night he died in Binnion, in 1709, it was said that devil tore a wall out of the house as he made off in haste with the unfortunate creature's soul. You couldn't imagine that happening to any of the Loughreys. As for the redoubtable Fr Edward, you'd never even know he'd been buried there, for part of his plan requested that his name would not be recorded on the Loughrey gravestone at Clonmany. His wishes were adhered to but the Binnion legend lives on.

Royal Sport of Cock Fighting

Tuesday 25 March and three following days

A main of 31 cocks and 10 Byes Between 16 Gentlemen of the City of Derry and County of Donegal. At 100 guineas a battle and a shake-bag battle on the last day at 50 Guineas each side!

From a Public Notice, 18 March 1783

The unfortunate birds were pitted against each other until there was one remaining – the winner. Birds were normally matched as equally as possible but the shake-bag appears to have been a luck-of-the-draw event. The money changing hands would amount to tens of thousands of pounds in today's world. In Derry there were three main gambling pursuits – horse racing, cards and cock-fighting, which was banned in 1835.

THE INCREDIBLE SKIPTONS

*A Duelling Cleric, a Marriage in Which No One Spoke
and a Runaway Bride*

Many generations ago the Skipton family was prominent in the affairs of Derry. The Skiptons owned vast amounts of property locally and there was talk of many amazing characters in the family. I was always intrigued by this but it was difficult to get any useful material on their background. Now, thanks to a manuscript found in the archives of Beech Hill House, much more is known about these incredible people. Their former abode is now the well-known Beech Hill Hotel just opposite Ardmore Chapel, about three miles from Derry.

So who were the Skiptons? Until recently all we knew was that they were a long–established family who lived at Beech Hill and had a grim-looking vault in Glendermott graveyard. One other fact was that a man with the extraordinary name of Pitt Skipton seemed to figure prominently in Derry of the mid-1800s. But in more modern times it seemed that the Skiptons had vanished from the face of the earth. This was until the recent discovery of what has come to be called *The Skipton Manuscript*. Now for the first time we can piece together the story of this intriguing local family who, as their offspring spread out, acquired huge amounts of land and numbers of houses around Derry, not to mention having considerable influence in the city's development.

The first fact that was revealed is that the Skiptons originally came to Ardmore about 1622, during the Plantation of Ulster and, having bought the townland of Ballyshaskey, they built Skipton Hall. During subsequent troubles, including the Siege of Derry, this dwelling was twice burned to the ground. The current house was built in 1738-9 by Captain Thomas Skipton. It was renamed Beech Hill on account of the many beech trees all around and soon this new residence was witness to some very odd happenings.

Firstly, Alexander Skipton, Thomas's son, became a clergyman after studying in Trinity College in Dublin in the 1730s. Shortly afterwards at a ball in Derry we find him in a fighting mood. It seems that a young officer refused to dance with his sister and this left him seething with rage. Cleric or not, Alexander Skipton demanded satisfaction by way of a duel and, unbelievably, chose a meeting place in the grounds of St Columb's Cathedral, not far from the main door. The belligerent Skipton shot the young officer dead, then quickly retreated to the safety of Beech Hill.

Some months later, this same Alexander got himself trapped in a most ridiculous love affair. It happened that after dinner in Beech Hill one evening the young men and women in the house retired to the drawing room to relax. By way of diversion they decided to stage a mock wedding. This apparently was a common entertainment of the day: the names of a boy and girl would be drawn from a hat and they would go through a version of the marriage ceremony. Then, after reading the vows, the pair would walk hand-in-hand to the applause and congratulations of the gathered assembly. As luck would have it, that evening the name of fiery Alexander Skipton was drawn along with that of Miss Isabella Kennedy, a beautiful young woman who had been brought up by the Tomkins family of Prehen. Apparently the gathering greatly enjoyed the mock wedding.

Then it appears that Alexander suddenly decided he really did love Isabella and wanted to marry her at a proper wedding. The girl's guardians at Prehen gave permission, only to find that Alexander had got cold feet and did not want to proceed with the ceremony. However, Mrs Rebecca Tomkins had other ideas and demanded that Skipton go through with the marriage and keep his word. Now it has to be said that at the best of times there was little love lost between the Skiptons and the Tomkins, so the forced nuptials led to unbelievable rows. These came to a head at supper on the wedding night when Alexander suddenly removed himself from the company and thenceforth refused to have anything to do with his new wife. Undaunted, Isabella took up residence at Beech Hill but not a word passed between the newly-weds.

Astonishingly, the stand-off at Beech Hill lasted for seven years. Husband and wife met in silence at the dinner table each evening. Then came a remarkable turnaround. At the foot of the staircase one night, Alexander, no doubt mellowed by a glass or two of wine, noticed a woman at the top of the stairs with what *The Skipton Manuscript* describes as, 'the most handsome pair of ankles he'd ever seen...' He asked if a new maid had been hired but was told that the ankles belonged to none other than his long-suffering wife Isabella. Seized with regret and no doubt with a generous measure of self-interest, Skipton sought reconciliation with Isabella, who is said to have cleverly replied, 'I have waited seven long years for you. Now you can wait the same for me.' However, it seems her heart eventually melted and the pair had several children, only one of whom survived.

Poor Isabella died in Beech Hill in 1776 and was the last Skipton to be buried in the ancient Glendermott graveyard on the old Lower Road before the erection of the new church on Church Brae, also built by the Skiptons. The couple's only surviving child, Thomas, was spoilt by his mother and became a virtual recluse at Beech Hill. A fastidious man, over-concerned with neatness and with his appearance, he could not tolerate noise and had a law passed that banned dogs from Ardmore for fear of hearing them bark. He married Elizabeth McCausland of Fruit Hill, Limavady, but all their children died before the father and Thomas bequeathed Beech Hill to his cousin George Kennedy, on condition that he would change his name to Skipton.

So Beech Hill had a new master in George Skipton, his family also being known as the Kennedy-Skiptons. George was elected to the Derry Corporation at the age of twenty-four and served as mayor in 1794 and 1795. During his time he replaced the old gates of Derry that were still there from the time of the Siege, saw to the refurbishment of the walls which had fallen into disrepair and began a much needed clean-up of the city streets. In a gesture hitherto unheard-of he invited the Catholic parish priest of the newly-built Ardmore Chapel to breakfast every Sunday morning – this at a time of rebellion in Ireland in the 1790s. At Beech Hill this became known as 'the priest's breakfast'.

Like his cousin of old, Alexander Skipton, George found himself embroiled in an impossible love tangle. The young woman in question was Sarah McCausland, whose sister Elizabeth had married Thomas Skipton of Beech Hill. George Skipton married Sarah in secret in Derry and she returned home to Fruit Hill, saying nothing to her mother, who was totally against the match. Sarah afterwards fled from Fruit Hill and mother and daughter didn't speak for years, until a dramatic reunion took place that would have put any Victorian penny dreadful in the shade. It was George who built the gloomy-looking Skipton vault at Glendermott and he was the first of the family to be laid to rest there.

The next person of interest in the family is George's sixth son, with the unusual name of Pitt Skipton. Pitt – the name comes from relatives of the Kennedys – appears to have been right at the heart of Derry's development as a commercial city in the 1800s. He was educated at Derry Free School in Bishop Street (the forerunner of Foyle College). Pitt comes across as a remarkable figure with a finger in many pies. I get the impression that he was a born speculator and that this was his Achilles' heel, if the truth be told. Some of his business ventures were successful but many were not – a fact hinted at in

The Skipton Manuscript.

Without a doubt Pitt Skipton's most significant contribution to Derry was the introduction of shipbuilding, in partnership with Dungiven man, John Henderson. Derry had no shipbuilding in the early 1800s. Any repairs were carried out by hauling the vessels from the Foyle into a crude dry dock cut into the riverbank. But in 1830, thanks to Skipton and Henderson, the city's first shipyard took shape in a site roughly the same as that now occupied by Tesco's on Strand Road. The first few years only repairs were carried out. Then in 1835, Derry's first ship, a brigantine called after the MP, Sir Robert Ferguson, was launched to great acclaim. The man overseeing the building of the vessel was none other than the brilliant Captain Coppin. But, as often happened with Pitt Skipton, he grew tired of his shipbuilding venture and sold the business to Coppin in 1839. Coppin was hailed as one of the city's brightest stars.

As for the mercurial Pitt Skipton, his new toy was the railway business. In the 1840s he joined the boards of both the Londonderry-Enniskillen Railway and the Londonderry-Coleraine Railway as secretary and director. This may well have been one of the ventures that failed, as the Coleraine Railway bankrupted its principal Derry investors due to massive construction problems. With the coming of the 1870s both Pitt and his second wife Sarah faded from the Derry scene.

This reminds me of a story I heard in Ardmore. Pitt, following in his father's liberal tradition, was friendly with the local parish priest, Patrick Mullan. The pair were under an oak tree one day and got to talking about the quality of wood for coffins. As a result Pitt had the oak cut down and steeped to make coffins for both of them. Father Mullan died young and his was the first of the coffins put to use.

As the 1800s progressed it seems to me as if the Skiptons lost their grip on Derry. The properties they had throughout the city, including the Waterside, were changing hands – even the Casino in Bishop Street built by Frederick Hervey, the Earl Bishop, and owned by the Skiptons, went under the hammer in 1869 to make way for St Columb's College. Most significant of all was that Beech Hill changed hands: it was bought in 1878 by Edward Nicholson, a highly successful railway engineer. Edward's rise to fame is a legend in itself but a story for another day. Finally, Beech Hill was to see a further change of ownership in 1989 when Patsy O'Kane and her brother Seamus Donnelly bought it in order to convert it into a hotel. They have worked tirelessly to maintain the traditions and elegance of a great country house.

For the record, *The Skipton Manuscript* was written in the Casino, Bishop Street, Derry, in 1849 by James Skipton, nephew of Pitt Skipton and grandson of George Kennedy-Skipton, who changed his name to inherit Beech Hill. The site of the Casino, given its name because of the Earl Bishop's fondness for Italy, is now Lumen Christi College.

FATE AND CAPTAIN BOGGS

...if it be not now, yet it will come...(Hamlet: V, ii)

Throughout the 1800s Derry was one of Ireland's great ports. Along Derry Quay, as it was known in song, you would have seen sailing ships – full-rigged vessels, schooners, clippers and barques – lined five abreast, some of them bound for far-off corners of the globe. While many of the ships carried produce, most of the voyages were for emigrants seeking passage to America, mainly to New York and Philadelphia. In the famine days of the 1840s thousands left Derry every year. Naturally, many weird and wonderful yarns came out of these great days of sail but there was none so odd as the strange tale of Captain Boggs.

Captain Robert Boggs of Derry's McCorkell Shipping Line was as resolute a man as ever you could hope to meet. A staunch Presbyterian, he was not the sort to get caught up in the quirky world of superstition, despite the fact that it seems to be the lot of most seafarers. But fate can play a waiting game and although Captain Boggs once stared death in the face and got away with it, superstitious Derry sailors knew his time would come. In the end it did – and with a vengeance.

I am reminded of a quotation in Shakespeare's *Hamlet*:

> *There's a special providence in the fall of a sparrow*
> *If it be now, 'tis not to come;*
> *if it be not to come, it will be now;*
> *if it be not now, yet it will come –*

There is a sinister feel to these words, something of a menacing inevitability, and certainly that's how it turned out to be for Robert Boggs.

Boggs was born in 1843 at Kilnappy, near Enagh, outside Derry, and grew up to be a lad of splendid character. He loved nothing more than to see the great sailing ships come and go from Derry Quay. It was no surprise then that he should beg his parents, Thomas and Mary, to let him go to sea, which eventually they did. His progress was steady and by 1879 he had his full master's ticket. At this stage he was given charge of the beautiful little McCorkell barque *Village Belle* – a much-loved vessel, with a black hull and white deck-houses, that plied the Atlantic between Derry and Philadelphia with passengers several times a year. Then on the strength of his success with the *Village Belle* Captain Boggs was asked by the McCorkell Line to take responsibility for Derry's pride and joy, the clipper *Minnehaha*. This certainly showed the regard in which Boggs was held. 'The safest pair of hands ever to sail a vessel from Derry Quay,' people said. Rumour had it in the taverns along the waterfront that a previous crew of the *Minnehaha* had been caught smuggling tobacco. The rock-solid Robert Boggs would never put up with that.

One cannot exaggerate the importance of the *Minnehaha*. Thousands travelled on her from Derry to New York between 1860 and 1875. Afterwards she served as a grain carrier until she was sold in 1895, after thirty-five years of sterling service. So popular was she that Derry people would line the banks of the River Foyle to see her come and go. The 'big green yacht', as she was popularly called, had her sleek hull painted in dark-green, with a gold stripe running just under her deck line and the deck itself was made of spotless honey-coloured pine. Crowning everything, on the prow was the figurehead of the mythical Native American girl Minnehaha – rather scantily clothed it must be added, apparently a tradition for sailing ships.

Everything went smoothly for Captain Boggs in the

Minnehaha until January 1884 when he set out with another Derry vessel, the *Nokomis,* for Baltimore on the eastern seaboard of America. Apparently there was a distinct feeling of unease along Derry Quay about this particular voyage. There had been trouble with stowaways, a fairly common occurrence, but bad as this was, something more sinister was niggling at the seafarers. A freak spring tide had left the Tuns sandbank at the entrance to Lough Foyle sitting up out of the water like a huge island. This was not a good omen. The Tuns is a three-mile-long stretch of crystal-white sand, lying roughly between Greencastle in County Donegal and Portstewart in County Derry. It has always been recognised as a major shipping hazard; great waves breaking over it at low tide create an awesome sight. The name 'Tuns' comes from the Irish word *tonn*, meaning wave. It is a place long associated with strange happenings such as mysterious lights and music; even the fairies are said to rest there occasionally. Most of all, tradition holds that Manannán Mac Lir, the spiteful Irish sea god, lies in wait at the Tuns in the hope of dragging ships to their doom. Small wonder then that folks in times past believed the Tuns was cursed.

In that January of 1884 the first odd thing we hear is that after leaving Derry port both vessels were becalmed at the mouth of the Foyle, in the spot known as Moville Roads near the port of Greencastle. There was not a breath of wind, unnatural for the time of year. More to the point, the *Minnehaha* and the *Nokomis* were just a stone's-throw from the terrifying Tuns. After seven days the ships did get away but immediately ran into difficulties in a fierce storm. In those days, leaving the Foyle against the prevailing south-west wind was dangerous at the best of times. Sailors made what was called their 'offing' (cleared the Scottish coastline) then tacked their way northwards in a curve towards America – a sickening, sometimes terrifying journey. Imagine what it was like in the teeth of a gale. Ships could spend weeks battling against the wind and the waves – and so it was with the *Minnehaha* and the *Nokomis* that January of 1884. Captain Murphy on the *Nokomis*, hearing his mast crack and with spars, rigging and sails tumbling down upon the deck, tucked the vessel in behind Tory Island for shelter.

Meanwhile the *Minnehaha* was taking an awful beating. Massive seas were breaking over her and it looked as if she would perish. But with disaster staring him in the face, whether by instinct or otherwise, Captain Boggs took a gamble. Instead of sheltering at Tory Island with the *Nokomis* he decided to run before the storm back towards Scotland. It was a colossal risk – he could easily have ended up on the rocky Scottish coastline. However, thanks to the *Minnehaha*'s versatility and Bogg's skill, he managed to turn the vessel without capsizing and, a little the worse for wear, she eventually reached the safety of the Clyde estuary.

What happened next was long to cast a dark shadow over Derry's days of sail. *Nokomis* limped back into the mouth of the Foyle and as a result of an unbelievable dispute about who should tow her to Derry she broke her moorings and was wrecked on the dreaded Tuns sandbank with the loss of all hands. How could a ship safely returned to its home river be lost? Was it fated to be? Did the sea god Manannán Mac Lir have his way? It is a story for another time, except to say that it caused outrage in Derry for years to come. But for some people it proved that the Tuns was a place of evil – able to claim a vessel when it took the notion to do so. And as for Captain Boggs, it was as if he had shaken his fist defiantly in the face of the Irish sea god, for if he had opted to remain with the *Nokomis* and returned to the Foyle the *Minnehaha* would surely have perished as well.

Overnight he was a hero. Soon the toast in Derry's quayside taverns was Captain Boggs, the gifted seaman whom Lady Luck had smiled upon. However, he would have none of it, believing that a good seaman relied on skill and experience. Luck had nothing to do with it as far as he was concerned. And so the superstitions of folk on Derry Quay were silenced as he continued to cross the seas successfully on the great *Minnehaha*. In all he had eight years service on the famous vessel and as a reward, in 1889, the McCorkells gave him a brand new cargo ship, the *Osseo*, the company's biggest ever vessel, built at Bigger's shipyard on the Foyle waterway.

Captain Boggs's voyages from Derry on the *Osseo* read like a round-the-world adventure: Montevideo, Rio de Janeiro, Philadelphia, San Francisco, Baltimore, ports in Australia and many other places. Yet astonishingly, in 1890, now aged forty-seven, he found the time to marry a girl called Sarah Campbell and promptly took her off to sea on his much-travelled ship. All the while fortune continued to smile on the Derry captain, as he now owned three houses in Derry and had valuable property in Australia.

In June 1892, after having been away for more than a year and a half, the *Osseo* came proudly sailing up the River Foyle to her much-loved home port. It was to be a short sojourn: in little more than a month she was away again to America but not before Mrs Sarah Boggs had been installed in a new home in Derry, with the couple's baby daughter, Mary, who had been born at sea. The captain was back in Derry in October 1892 and then again in May 1893. During that year he had become the proud father of a son, Samuel. In August, once more, the *Osseo* was off. This time she was on a world trip – North America, South America and across to Australia via South Africa; then once more to South America and finally back to Falmouth, where she arrived early in December 1894.

The next news of her was on 17 December 1894, when she was about to battle up the Irish Sea in a gale. Word reaching Derry by telegraph was that she was bound for Ardrossan in Scotland to discharge cargo before heading for her home port on the Foyle. Naturally relatives of the crew were overjoyed that their loved ones would soon be berthing at Derry Quay. But it was not to be. The gales got so vicious that half-way up the Irish Sea Captain Boggs felt he should shelter at Holyhead. At this stage we must rely on reports from the scene of the catastrophe that was about to unfold.

At 3.45am on the morning of 31 December 1894, the Holyhead lighthouse keeper saw the *Osseo* making for the outer harbour, which was protected by a breakwater. Normally the manoeuvre past the breakwater would have been straightforward for a mariner of Bogg's experience. But now I return to my earlier quotation: 'If it be not now, yet it will come...' Suddenly a gigantic wave washed the *Osseo* against the breakwater, smashing the vessel clean in two. All hands were lost. Providence had deemed that the time had come for Captain Robert Boggs. Those of the crew who were not killed by falling masts were washed from the deck into the raging seas; the remains of the vessel were submerged within minutes. So almost ten years after his great escape, Captain Robert Boggs met the watery grave that had eluded him on the raging Tuns at the mouth of the Foyle. Fate had caught up with him. One imagines it was no surprise to the superstitious sailors who had gathered on Derry Quay as word came in from Holyhead, for this is often the way with seafarers: they are resigned to whatever fate the sea decrees.

Naturally the entire community was aghast at the news and it is true to say that the loss of the *Osseo* put an end to Derry's great days of sail. One bright star amid the gloom was that Sarah Boggs was still there to care for their two children. And while Captain Boggs did not live to see his son Samuel grow up, the boy lived to continue the name of Boggs. Today the Boggs family can proudly look back to their seafaring ancestor, one of Derry's greatest sea captains. Perhaps the words of the poet Longfellow, who was so close to the heart of Derry ship owner Barry McCorkell, leave us with a fitting memory of Captain Robert Boggs:

> *In spite of rocks and tempest roar,*
> *In spite of false lights on the shore,*
> *Sail on, nor fail to breast the sea!*
> *Our hearts, our hopes, are all with thee.*

One strange postscript: just three days before Captain Boggs perished on the *Osseo*, odd to relate, his former great ship the *Minnehaha* had also sought shelter in Holyhead. It was a weird coincidence. Then during a lull in the storm her captain decided to make a run down the Irish Sea. So there is every chance that Captain Boggs would have caught a glimpse of his former vessel as he made his way up to Holyhead. Did the ships pass in the night, one wonders – the grand old *Minnehaha* journeying safely away, while the *Osseo* sailed on to her doom?

The rather odd names of the McCorkell vessels generate much interest. They are native-American names and it came about like this. Barry McCorkell was sent off to sea to learn the shipping business as a young man. It was while travelling the eastern seaboard of America that he met the poet H.W. Longfellow and became fascinated by his works. By the time the famous 'Song of Hiawatha' was published in the 1850s, Barry McCorkell had become established as the head of the company and opted to name his future ships after characters in the Longfellow poem: *Minnehaha* – sometimes called Laughing Water but more correctly Waterfall – *Nokomis* – Daughter of the Moon – and *Osseo* – Son of the Evening Star. Sadly, three ships with Indian names from the Hiawatha poem were lost with all hands – the *Owenee*, the *Nokomis* and the *Osseo*.

C.W. Gordon: *Reminiscences of Derry in the Mid-1800s*

I was born in 1858 and in my time I have crossed three Derry bridges – the old Wooden Bridge, Carlisle Bridge and Craigavon Bridge. As a boy coming from school I would pass by way of Clarendon Street and from thence to Derry Quay. Here I would gaze in awe at the large wooden vessels owned by McCorkells. These vessels, once proud passenger ships, would soon be taking timber and grain from America. I remember two of them very well – the Village Belle and the Minnehaha. The Village Belle was commanded by Captain Little, whose home was in Prince's Street and the Minnehaha by Captain McGrath. I looked longingly through the portholes at the bunks inside and in my youthful simplicity wished I too could take passage to America.

C.W. Gordon belonged to a dynasty that owned one of Derry's long-established stores: Gordon's of the Diamond. Incidentally, like many shop-owners of the time, the family lived above the premises. C.W. Gordon published these reminiscences in 1945, at the age of eighty-seven. His insight is interesting as there are very few accounts by people who actually witnessed the great sailing ships on Derry Quay.

Roll Up for the Big Bang!

How the Mussenden Temple Stood Firm

The Derry–Belfast railway line came into being in 1845 amid controversy, bankruptcy and the biggest explosion ever heard in Ireland. But the question on everyone's mind was: would tunnelling under the Mussenden Temple in Downhill on the coast of County Derry cause the venerable old edifice to go crashing down into the sea?

It's a miracle we ever had a rail link at all in the north-west of Ireland. The present track, which now runs to Belfast, was first proposed in 1844 and was intended only to reach Coleraine. Even at that it took nearly ten years to complete. From the beginning of the enterprise there were construction difficulties, disputes, bankruptcies and sackings. No surprise then that there were frequent calls for the entire scheme to be abandoned. All these problems stemmed from the choice of route to get the railway the thirty miles to Coleraine from Derry. The original engineers felt it was better to hug the Lough Foyle shoreline and then go through the cliff in Downhill at the ocean's edge than to have to negotiate the mountainous area around Limavady.

Two outstanding men, the architect Charles Lanyon (later Sir Charles) and the engineer Robert Stephenson, made this controversial decision. Lanyon, a brilliant builder and surveyor, is credited with shaping much of Belfast as we know it today, while Stephenson helped his famous father, George, to design the first railway locomotives, including the world-renowned 'Rocket'. Lanyon and Stephenson carried out the initial surveys early in 1845 and envisaged few difficulties. Such optimism was not surprising: these were the days of the railway boom, when engineers felt they could conquer any obstacle. Little did they realise the problems that lay ahead.

In the first place the beautiful Mussenden Temple, built in 1783, sat proudly on the Downhill cliff-top, facing the Atlantic, and the railway would go through a tunnel about a hundred feet underneath. Undoubtedly this was a gamble, for it would require extensive blasting. Yet the engineers were undaunted and to show their confidence brought two hundred miners in from England to assist with the task. Apart from the Mussenden Temple, another bone of contention had been conveniently put to the side – the reclamation of part of Lough Foyle. This was to enable the building of a line-of-sight track between Derry and Downhill. An embankment was required and many wondered if such a structure would stand the test of wind and tide. As it happened, the fears were justified, for the worst weather in living memory was about to strike.

Nonetheless, great excitement greeted the launching of the new railway project in the spring of 1845. Derry had always been an isolated city, so townsfolk viewed the railway as a major bonus, if not a necessity. Affairs on the ground were to be monitored by a local committee, while a London-based company would manage finance and general business. Thus was born the Londonderry and Coleraine Railway (L&C). In the summer of 1845 the reclamation of Lough Foyle's eastern shore got underway. This was done at different sites in order to demonstrate that the undertaking was possible. But in truth all eyes were on the cliff face at Downhill where initial drilling for the tunnel was about to begin.

That November the Mussenden Temple got its first test. A horizontal shaft was required for initial operations on the cliff-face and this necessitated the use of explosives to open the way. People watched anxiously as Lady Bruce, wife of the owner of the land, lit the fuse and a modest charge was set off. Happily no damage was done, the temple stood firm and everyone heaved a sigh of relief. So far so good – but it was early days.

It occurs to me, whenever I contemplate the cliff and the temple, to wonder if Frederick Hervey, Earl of Bristol and Bishop of Derry, was turning in his grave with all that was going on. He had built the monument as a memorial for his young ward and sweetheart, Fridiswide Mussenden, and got the idea when he first glimpsed the Temple of Vesta at Tivoli outside Rome. Incidentally, the name Fridiswide was that of the patron saint of Oxford.

If anyone thought the detonation of the small charge by Lady Bruce was all there was to it they were in for a big surprise – the threat to the Mussenden Temple wasn't over by a long way. In June 1846 the engineers calculated that 30,000 tons of rock would have to be removed from the cliff-face to provide access to the tunnel. It called for something gigantic in the line of blasting – a ton of explosive – and all of this would be planted underneath the famous temple. The like of it had never been heard of before. Nerves jangled as people looked gingerly up at the classical edifice on the cliff edge. Then something happened that might have been a massive folly. In their wisdom the builders decided that the general public should see their tunnelling handiwork. The detonation of the explosive was publicised as if it were to be the greatest show on earth. For weeks before it was advertised in carnival fashion in newspapers and on posters:

The Big Bang! An explosion to end all explosions!

The like of it had ever been seen or heard. Hundreds arrived. Special excursion transport had been arranged: there were jaunting cars and carriages from Derry, Coleraine and Limavady and boatloads of people came from Moville across Lough Foyle. All eyes were on the Mussenden Temple. Would it disappear into the sea? The excitement was unbearable. Then, with everyone pushed back from the scene and amid loud cheers from the crowd, the massive charge was detonated.

Accounts tell of a noise like thunder echoing between the Downhill cliffs on the County Derry shore and the Donegal hills opposite for what seemed an eternity. Some witnesses said that even the skies darkened. What followed was an amazing sight. At first the 30,000 tons of rock slipped slowly from the cliff face in one piece. The rock went quietly in the beginning but then it gathered pace and with an angry roar it entered the sea with an almighty crash, creating a mini tidal wave.

For a moment there was silence. The fate of the temple was unknown, as a pall of black smoke lay across the entire area like a thick blanket. Then out of the gloom someone spotted the revered edifice on the cliff-top still intact. There it was, defiantly staring out to sea, having withstood the mighty blast. The biggest explosion ever to take place in Ireland had not dislodged it. Three cheers went up for the temple, more by way of relief than jubilation. Then, in celebration, the miners held a party inside the tunnel itself. One observer described it as a bizarre scene, resembling Dante's *Inferno*. The place was lit with lamps and candles and there were makeshift chandeliers dangling from the ceiling. Gunpowder smoke lay everywhere like a thick curtain of mist and the miners were staggering about, very much the worse for drink. For weeks afterwards there were tales of alcoholic miners still lost in the tunnel and eerie cries for help. Later, work began on a smaller tunnel but the excitement was over, as the Mussenden Temple was not near this part of the operation.

But problems were not over for the railway. In fact, they were only beginning. Trouble arose with the efforts to reclaim the Lough Foyle shoreline by means of an embankment. It would run on the shoreline between Coolkeeragh, just outside Derry, and Magilligan Point, a distance of some fifteen miles, and enable a massive 20,000 acres of land to be recovered. It soon became apparent that this was easier said than done. Lough Foyle stubbornly refused to give up the land it covered. Tides breached the embankment frequently; there was large-scale flooding and the company doing the work was forced to quit. A succession of contractors and engineers failed to solve the problems and the dreadful winter weather compounded the situation. As late as 1849 affairs were still in a disastrous condition. Things were so bad that when the famous writer Thomas Carlyle visited Derry that same year and viewed the embankment he commented: 'This is an attempted futility!'

One man who thought he could solve the problems and get the railway up and working in the late 1840s and 1850s was William McCormick. He was a self-made Derry man whose fortune came from building railways in England. Yet the storms and the hostile conditions of his own locality defeated him and he was declared bankrupt in a very short time. Having been almost a millionaire, when he died he had only £100 in the bank, thanks to the L&C Railway. Eventually, the Derry-Coleraine rail link did open, though not before it dented the careers of many engineers and emptied the pockets of several investors. By 1853 it was fully functional and you could travel return from Derry to Coleraine for four shillings if you fancied a basic third-class compartment. Some years later it was remarked that a strange little quirk had occurred with regard to employment on the railway. Somehow the number four was predominating. The records for 1856 show that there were four clerks, four engine drivers, four firemen, four guards and four pointsmen – however, strangely, there were thirteen stationmasters.

Back to the Mussenden Temple. It's now more than a hundred and sixty years since the day of the 'big bang', and the striking old building still stands, unflustered by what happened back in 1846. The Latin inscription from Lucretius (*c*. 99-55BC) around the Temple frieze remains enigmatic. Roughly translated it reads: 'How satisfying it is to see others in trouble amid the storms knowing it's not you.'

It looks as if there was more to the Earl of Bristol than people ever gave him credit for.

DERRY'S AIR-CRASH RIDDLE

Young Pilot's Last Letter Home

There is a tree-lined field in Ardmore just outside Derry that greets each winter season with a quiet sadness. This lonely patch of earth just a few yards from St Mary's Church harbours a strange stillness, a sense of hush. This feeling of quiet sadness is quite fitting, for herein lies a tale of grief, of mystery and of many broken hearts. It was at this spot on Friday morning, 27 February 1948, in cold, foggy weather, that a Hawker Sea Fury aeroplane, a fighter-bomber, ploughed headlong into the earth, killing its pilot. Hundreds flocked from Derry to the crash site to stare at the engine lying in a pool of oil and see the thirty-yard gash on the ground made by the impact of the aircraft – a Fleet Air Arm plane out of Eglinton, County Derry, it was said, with a popular young pilot. Little else was known. Now, in an amazing twist of fate, much more light can be thrown on that air crash of bygone times. Strange to relate a last letter from the young pilot to his parents written shortly before his death has come to light and after all these years it has still left us with a mystery.

Firstly, to the aftermath of the crash itself. The following day, Saturday 28 February, 1948, the *Derry Journal* covered the inquest and gave the pilot's name as John Lewis Edwin Prendy, a twenty-two-year-old London lad. A later report said his mother had arrived in Derry for the funeral, accompanied by her son-in-law. John was laid to rest at St Canice's Church, Eglinton, alongside young men who had died just a few years before in the Second World War. After that the incident was forgotten, buried in the mists of time. However, the Prendys have been regular visitors to the Eglinton grave and treasured memories of the talented young pilot live on vividly with his family. It is through these recollections that we are able to get a picture of John Prendy and the remarkable letter he sent home before the fatal crash.

John was born near Edgware in London in 1925, the first son of Lewis and Dorothy Prendy. He attended the excellent Jesuit-run St Ignatius College, whose students included George Martin of Beatles fame and the movie genius Alfred Hitchcock. John was a highly talented, charming young man, excelling at football and athletics. He was also very good-looking and, along with his affable nature, this made him a heart-throb with the girls. But it seems girlfriends were always brought home for his mother's approval. Above everything young Prendy dreamed of becoming a pilot and after air-cadet training and stints in America and Canada he was attached to the Fleet Air Arm Anti-Submarine Base at HMS Gannet, Eglinton, in 1947.

He was now twenty-two and I think the idea of marriage must always have been to the fore with him. Among his many admirers were a delightful London girl called Thelma and the gifted opera singer, Sylvia Dando. But out of the blue, early in 1947, John met a girl here in the north-west and by Christmas he was well and truly in love with her. As we shall see, mystery surrounds this young woman who had captured his heart.

We know of her only because the purpose of John Prendy's last letter to his parents was to tell them he was getting engaged. John posted this letter in Eglinton on the evening of Wednesday, 25 February 1948 and the following night he telephoned his mother to calm her fears about his sudden engagement. Sadly it proved to be his last contact with home, for the fatal crash occurred the following morning, Friday 27 February. That same Friday afternoon a telegram boy knocked on the door of John's parents in London and brought the chilling news that their son had been killed just hours earlier in an air accident outside Derry; his funeral would be held on Tuesday 2 March 1948, at St Canice's Church, Eglinton; third-class tickets for rail and boat would be issued if they wished to attend. It was as brief as that. The fact that John's letter arrived after his death makes it all the more moving. In it a son's respect for his parents shines brightly in every word and he jokes about the engagement;

> You'll probably think I'm a bit round the bend…and I know you'll say I've said it all before…but honestly we're serious…It'll be in May and I want you all there.

And he finishes

> I'll explain all…Don't worry about anything.
> Your loving son,
> John

It is a strange quirk of fate that this letter was speeding on its way to his parents as John's fatal accident was taking place.

Surprisingly, the Prendy family never really knew the exact details of the crash but from various archives I have been able to build up a picture of what happened on the fateful day. It had been very cold so conditions were wintry as the Hawker Sea Fury took off from Eglinton in mid-morning on that Friday. These routine flights generally kept to the country districts and around noon people watching from Drumahoe village, three miles from Derry, saw smoke coming from the plane's engine, which had begun to make a strange noise. The trouble was serious, for John Prendy made no attempt to return to Eglinton, just a few miles away. Soon the aircraft began to lose height and was seen to make for a large sloping field opposite the nearby Ashbrook estate. But at several tons in weight and with power failing, the Sea Fury struck trees during the descent and hurtled headlong into the ground. Wreckage scattered everywhere and although the fuselage remained partly intact the pilot was killed on impact.

Two onlookers and a nurse made an attempt to render assistance to the pilot but the remains of the aeroplane caught fire and made it impossible to approach it. However, within minutes, firemen were on the scene, alerted by a colleague of John's who was circling in the air overhead. Afterwards personnel from the Eglinton base arrived to undertake the grim task of tidying up but the nature of the engine fault was never disclosed.

Now to the mysterious sweetheart whom John met locally. Who was she? The only clue we have is revealed in John's last letter where he says: 'I first met Barbara here (in Derry) early in 1947...' So did John Prendy meet this girl called Barbara when out socialising in the city or elsewhere? Derry had been bustling with all nationalities during the war and was still vibrant in 1947–8. Without a doubt, John would have been familiar with the popular dance halls and the pubs and clubs here. Was Barbara a local girl, a country girl, or perhaps not from here at all? John's younger brother Tony is in no doubt that John telephoned his mother the night before the tragedy to say he was marrying an Irish girl.

One thing we can imagine is that Barbara was inconsolable at the funeral, her name added to the ever-growing list of broken hearts that comprised John's family and his many admirers. Yet this girl remains a mystery. There is no information on what happened to her afterwards or even if she is now alive or dead. Something we do know is that John Prendy loved the Derry locality and the north-west of Ireland. All reports talk of his absolute passion for planes and his love of flying in this part of the world. Perhaps that is no surprise – solo flyers hereabouts tell me that the supreme beauty of the Donegal hills and the Sperrin Mountains, divided by the majestic sweep of the River Foyle winding around Derry, give unmatched panoramas from the air.

John Prendy, like many of the early young pilots, quite

literally lived to get into the air. The Italian writer Daniele del Giudice says flying creates a world of its own – up among the clouds – a different, disconnected existence with a peculiar adrenaline rush. A Canadian Air Force pilot, J.G. Magee, who was killed seven years before John Prendy, reflected on this sheer joy of flying with a poem called 'High Flight':

> *Oh, I have slipped the surly bonds of earth*
> *And danced the skies on laughter-silvered wings.*
> *Sunward I've climbed and joined the tumbling*
> *Mirth of sun-split clouds, and done a hundred*
> *Things you have not dreamed of…*

Yet Daniele del Giudice adds that subconsciously all aviators realise that engine trouble or even one simple error can be a prelude to disaster.

There is also an echo of John Prendy's fate in W.B. Yeats's poem about a young Irish aviator who foresees his death:

> *I know that I shall meet my fate*
> *Somewhere among the clouds above…*

Many of the early aviators were seen to live only for the moment – for the sheer ecstasy of flying, even though they sensed that death lay waiting. As for John Prendy, there is not the slightest sign in his last letter that he foresaw tragedy ahead or that he had any presentiment of death. His writing is relaxed, his words happy and optimistic, his future wedding plans well to the fore. I can only conclude that his Hawker aircraft's Centaurus engine, usually seen to be most reliable, developed a catastrophic fault, and as fate would have it trees were in the way as he attempted an emergency landing. An Ancient Greek saying comes to mind: 'Those whom the gods love die young.'

Sadly, the crash saw the demise of a gifted and charming young man – one of those times when a youthful light went out well and truly. And it has left us with an enduring riddle. Was the Shakespearean inscription (from *As You Like It*) on John's headstone a farewell message to his sweetheart?

> *Hereafter in a better world than this,*
> *I hope to have more love and knowledge of you.*

If so, who was this mysterious Barbara who had stolen young Prendy's heart?

Jim Donaghy, 'Going Home From the War', in Gardiner S. Mitchell's *Three Cheers for the Derrys!*

I sent a telegram to my mother to tell her I was on my way home. When I arrived at the Waterside station there was no one there to meet me so I started the long walk to Drumahoe. As I walked down Daly's brae in my uniform, someone must have spotted me in the distance. The bell of Clarke's Mill at Drumahoe started ringing frantically as a signal to my mother that I was back. When I got there the house was filled with my friends, relations and neighbours. They were overjoyed.

Jim Donaghy, who was twenty-one years old at the time, was returning home from the Great War. It was just after Christmas 1918 and he had travelled from Germany, through Denmark, to Scotland and then Larne. Jim had been at the Battle of the Somme, having joined the 10th Royal Inniskilling Fusiliers (the 'Derrys') and lost many young friends in the resulting carnage. Clarke's Mill, near Drumahoe village, was driven by a millstream fed by the River Faughan. The mill bell was sounded by Mrs Hughes, who lived in the mill and was watching out for Jim coming down the brae after his three-mile walk from the Waterside

WHAT BECKONING GHOST...?

The Beresford Ghost

'...A Touch that Was as Cold as Death Itself'

I admit to being quite chauvinistic about the north-west but I'm convinced that it is no boast to claim for it one of the most famous ghost stories in Ireland. The tale of the man who returned from death is usually referred to as the 'Beresford Ghost' and it's only recently that I uncovered the local connection in among some dusty old records. Make no mistake about it, this is a spooky tale, and the fact that it started on our own doorstep makes it all the more spine-chilling. It does appear to be a genuine haunting. I had heard about the Beresford Ghost years ago. What I didn't realise then was that it all began at Walworth, near Ballykelly, just a few miles from Derry. Now nothing pleases me more than a bit of ghost-hunting, so I set out enthusiastically to see what I could uncover about this famous local tale.

It was October, the month of Hallowe'en, and I couldn't have chosen a darker day. My first stop was the beautiful old-world residence of Walworth Lodge, barely a mile from Ballykelly village. It's built on the site of a much older house and bawn dating back to the Plantation. It's here, so the story goes, that a sinister pact was made between two young people in the late 1600s. The pair involved were John, Lord Tyrone, and Nicola Sophia Hamilton, both barely twenty years of age and inseparable friends from childhood. Grisly as it sounds, they promised to return from death; whoever died first was to come back and relate what things were like beyond the grave.

From all I have heard, something mighty weird did take

place. So, having arrived at Ballykelly, I carefully went over my notes to see if I could make sense of what really did happen. It seems that Nicola forgot completely about the pact and eventually married a landowner, Sir Tristram Beresford. However, it was not long after this that strange things began to occur and it all started with a visit by Nicola to her sister at Gill Hall in County Down. Out of nowhere, in the middle of the night, Nicola's childhood friend John suddenly appeared at her bedside, saying he had died and had returned from death to honour his promise. The petrified girl babbled that it must be a dream but the apparition was soon to prove otherwise. Apparently he did describe what life was like after death and went on to make several frightening prophecies. Firstly, he told Nicola that she would soon have a son but that her husband would die shortly afterwards. Next he said that she would marry again into great unhappiness and that her own death would come at the beginning of the forty-seventh year of her life.

But the ghost hadn't finished. Amid Nicola's protests that this must be an awful nightmare, he caused the drapes around the four-poster to rise and fold over on top of the bed canopy. Then he wrote his signature in her pocket book and finally he placed his hand upon her wrist with a touch that was as cold as death itself. It wasn't the sort of night visitor you would wish on anybody and naturally enough the effect on Nicola was devastating. The following day she appeared with a black ribbon round her wrist where the ghost had touched her. Later she fell into a fit of despair when news did indeed arrive that John, Lord Tyrone, had died two days earlier.

One by one the ghost's prophecies came true. Nicola gave birth to a son and then her husband died. She now began to lead an isolated life, hoping to avoid a second marriage, but she eventually gave in to the persistent pleas of a young officer and the pair were wed. They frequently resided here in the north-west, with poor Nicola steeped in a life of anguish and misery, constantly fretting about the ghost's prophecies.

Then one day she suddenly appeared much happier than she had been for years. Announcing that it was her birthday, she summoned a few friends together to celebrate, and gave an explanation of sorts. She said she that a dark cloud had suddenly been lifted from her life as she had now reached the age of forty-eight. There were toasts all round but suddenly an old minister rose to speak, 'You do yourself a disservice ma'am,' said he. 'It was I who baptised you and I can say without contradiction that you are only forty-seven.'

Remembering the ghost's awful prophecy Nicola was stunned; she thought she had outlived the fateful age of forty-seven. 'If it is so, if I am only forty-seven this day, then you have signed my death warrant,' she gasped. With that she withdrew in shock to her bedroom and sent for her children. There she recounted the bizarre tale of what had happened at Gill Hall all those years before. One of the odd features she stressed was the ghost's cold aloofness – so strange in someone who had been her childhood friend.

Nicola died inexplicably that very evening. It's said that when then black ribbon was removed there was a deep imprint of a thumb on her wrist and the sinews were withered to the bone.

But back to my search at Ballykelly. I found Walworth to have very much a lived-in feel about it. I walked around the complete demesne and it was easy to imagine John and Nicola sitting before a big open fire of a winter's evening, sharing their views about life after death. But why was the ghost so cold and remote when he appeared to Nicola, I wondered, and what did he really say about the afterlife? Nearby, I found the ruin of the church built by the Hamiltons in the 1600s. Nicola may have been baptised here and she and John would have strolled the paths hereabouts when they were growing up. Perhaps it was here that they first conceived the seeds of their dreadful pact.

But how much of this strange yarn can we believe? Andrew Lang, the celebrated Scots writer on ghosts, felt that Nicola imagined it all and pointed to the fact that there have been similar stories in other countries. However, there is the tradition in Ireland of the so-called 'death nip' – when people find unexplained bruises on their arms that sometimes resemble thumb or finger impressions and are said to be made by the dead.

As for Nicola, her last resting place is in St Patrick's Cathedral, Dublin. Her portrait with the black ribbon on her wrist could be seen in the Beresfords' Dublin house until it was sold many decades ago. Some people say that the picture then vanished mysteriously but others maintain it still hangs in Howth Castle. At the ruins of the old church at Walworth I was conscious of a strange feeling of melancholy. Maybe it was induced by the October half-light or perhaps it was because I knew it was the anniversary of the ghost's appearance. By the way, Sir Walter Scott felt the story was good enough to give it a mention in one of his poems and it's believed that the Waterford branch of the Beresford family still have the pocket book with the ghost's signature. One thing is certain: there can be no more spooky goings-on at Gill Hall, no more journeys from beyond the grave, for the grim edifice was mysteriously burned to the ground in 1969.

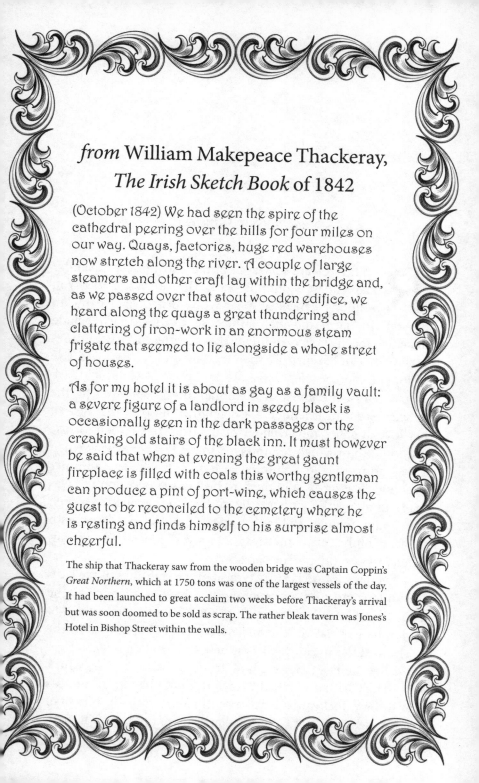

from William Makepeace Thackeray, *The Irish Sketch Book* of 1842

(October 1842) We had seen the spire of the cathedral peering over the hills for four miles on our way. Quays, factories, huge red warehouses now stretch along the river. A couple of large steamers and other craft lay within the bridge and, as we passed over that stout wooden edifice, we heard along the quays a great thundering and clattering of iron-work in an enormous steam frigate that seemed to lie alongside a whole street of houses.

As for my hotel it is about as gay as a family vault: a severe figure of a landlord in seedy black is occasionally seen in the dark passages or the creaking old stairs of the black inn. It must however be said that when at evening the great gaunt fireplace is filled with coals this worthy gentleman can produce a pint of port-wine, which causes the guest to be reconciled to the cemetery where he is resting and finds himself to his surprise almost cheerful.

The ship that Thackeray saw from the wooden bridge was Captain Coppin's *Great Northern*, which at 1750 tons was one of the largest vessels of the day. It had been launched to great acclaim two weeks before Thackeray's arrival but was soon doomed to be sold as scrap. The rather bleak tavern was Jones's Hotel in Bishop Street within the walls.

THE LAVENDER LADY

Suddenly She Vanished...

Recently I went in search of the ghost of the Lavender Lady at St Columb's Park House, Waterside. You wouldn't expect a spirit with such a nice name to do you any harm and that is the case. But it doesn't exclude mischief, for the lady certainly makes her presence felt at times – as we'll hear. No surprise then that her antics have given rise to lots of spooky tales. Most stories about St Columb's Park House tell of the ghost of a woman always followed by the delicate scent of lavender – a delightful notion – because of her love of gathering lavender plants from the garden for use indoors. All of which reminds me that a few years back when I was admiring St Columb's Park House late one summer evening, a passer-by told me how he had seen the ghost. 'I was walking along the path in the garden,' he recalled, '...when this young woman suddenly appeared out of nowhere, with a basket on her arm and dressed in a very old-fashioned way. Then just as suddenly she vanished.'

That description is fairly typical of the sightings of the lady. To understand what's happening you have to go back to the early days of this lovely dwelling. The wonderfully wooded St Columb's Park sits in the ancient lands of Clooney, from the Irish word for 'meadows'. It was here in 1788 that naval officer John Rea built an elegant bow-fronted manor house, which he called 'Chatham' after the town in Kent, then known for its Royal Navy dockyards and as a centre for the refurbishment of vessels. Rea left us St Columb's Park, as we now know it, with its sixty acres of oak, beech and lime trees and delightful vistas. In the early 1800s, his granddaughter, barely eighteen years of age, married Sir George Hill of Brookhall, Culmore, and the house was renamed St Columb's after the little church nearby. Sir George's wife died young but the Hills remained until 1889, when Joseph Cooke of Derry shipping fame took up residence there with his family. The Cookes' sojourn lasted almost three decades.

By the 1930s the place was empty save for a caretaker and in 1937 it was vested by Londonderry Corporation. US Army officers used the house during the Second World War and later it became a nurses' home for the local TB hospital. Finally, after another vacant period, the building was completely refurbished in 1994 and became the acclaimed reconciliation centre we know today. Somewhere during those two hundred years or so there was a tragic incident at the house, an incident so sad, so traumatic, that it stamped itself forever in people's memory of this beautiful place.

For clues as to when this happened and who the Lavender Lady might be, we have to study the description of the ghost. Her appearance is Victorian in style – a flowing dress in soft colours reaching right down to her feet – and by all accounts she is definitely not an old person. This means that we must look at the early days of St Columb's Park House, possibly when John Rea was still alive and most likely during the early years of the union between the Reas and the Hills of Brookhall. Having often been through the house – even before the present refurbishment – my impression is that the Lavender Lady is a very sad ghost. You get this feeling of melancholy on the landings and stairs, a gentle sort of resigned sadness, a softness in the air; indeed, you can almost imagine a faint sigh at times.

One bedroom in particular is associated with the ghost. It's a delightful room, incidentally, decorated in lavender, with a fine bow window in the Georgian style. Looking out from this window takes you right back to those early times: the beeches and the oaks of St Columb's beyond compare and the view across the River Foyle breathtaking. But, so the story goes, on a bleak far-off day, tragedy struck, with the death of a young woman at this spot. Reports that she took her own life are unclear and unproven yet the tale lives on.

As for the sightings of the ghost, you can trace manifestations over the past years and these are much the same as recent reports: Hallowe'en is a favourite time for appearances. Not long ago the lights and some cooking appliances came on one evening, apparently of their own accord. On another occasion a vase was seen to slide across the mantelpiece as if guided by an unseen hand. And it seems that sounds – some very loud – are frequently heard when no one is there.

It's intriguing that the smell of lavender accompanies all these unusual occurrences. Yet the Lavender Lady makes very few appearances in person. She has been seen on the landing and in the garden at the front of the house, but not all that often. This leads me to conclude that what she is really doing is keeping a watchful eye on the place. The odd sightings are nothing more than little reminders that she hasn't gone away.

Strangely enough, a visit from some psychics a few years ago revealed that there might be more than one ghost at St Columb's and a young boy in Victorian garb has been seen walking past one of the downstairs windows. Who knows, maybe this lad has been up to some pranks, like the sudden unexplained opening of doors and the many weird and wild noises. All in all, my latest visit left me with the impression of a rather sorrowful spirit. It is perhaps the ghost of a young lady surrounded by some of her kith and kin: gentle in her ways, a lover of nature and in particular of the special aroma of lavender. As Hallowe'en approaches each autumn one cannot help wonder (and even hope?) if the Lavender Lady will appear again to unburden her sadness in the beautiful setting of St Columb's Park House?

Thirteen Steps

A Haunting at the Waterside Workhouse

Is there a ghost at the old Waterside Workhouse on Derry's Glendermott Road? I firmly believe there is and I went back there recently, wondering if I might get a sighting of the tormented spirit known as the 'Matron in Blue'. A strange incident in the 1920s provides a clue about this ghost, which is said to haunt the stairways and corridors of the broody old building, eternally regretting some past wickedness. More of that later. But first I emphasise again that there is something in the atmosphere of this workhouse that, like many others, was built in 1841. You can sense it – a sort of uneasy stillness, a feeling that the very stones in the walls hold memories that want to reveal themselves to you. Certainly you do not want to be in this place on your own. I assure you it is decidedly eerie. Though much of the old workhouse has gone, there remains enough of the original structure in the little on-site museum to remind you of the bad old days and certainly what remains does look extremely grisly.

The first thing that sets you thinking about weird happenings is the discovery that there are thirteen steps up to the workhouse door. I wondered about that strange coincidence. These are the very steps that saw thousands of Derry's hapless poor come and go for more than a hundred years. You can imagine the hopeless misery that possessed them and perhaps it's no surprise that the steps are intricately connected with my ghost story. I suppose I may as well also admit to you that I have not managed to track down the Matron in Blue in over thirty years of searching. Yes, I have been on her track for all that time! My first visit was many decades ago when I was given permission to take photographs in the building, then completely empty and undisturbed since 1947.

Back then, as darkness was falling, one of the places I stumbled upon was the old dispensary. The door was lying off its hinges and with my heart pounding I felt an awful sense of dread. Was there something lurking inside? I've thought about it ever since. There were no windows in this empty, drab, oppressive, little room and had I known then what I know now I would not have lingered another second. You see this place, this little room, held the key to the gruesome tale of the Matron in Blue. It was firmly believed that the apparition of a nurse dressed in an old-fashioned blue uniform was frequently seen in the Waterside Hospital, which had come into being in the 1940s as the workhouse was being phased out. However, it seems that this spirit was often spotted in much earlier times in the main body of the workhouse and had then been given the sinister name of 'Matron in Blue'.

Reports of the sightings of this unfortunate being always depict a woman in distress, fretting and moving rapidly through the wards and dark passageways, as if searching for something. The vision has been described as hair-raising, to say the least. The description of the matron's blue uniform with a sort of white pinafore dates her to the late Victorian period, say just before 1900, and over the years I have gradually been able to put the pieces of this ghostly tale together.

In bygone times workhouses could be cruel places in the extreme; the master and the matron ruled with absolute authority. And as luck would have it there arrived in the Waterside workhouse before the turn of the 1900s a matron whose hard-heartedness exceeded all bounds.

These were days when inmates still broke stones or stitched mailbags and lay side by side at night in their hundreds in unspeakable conditions. It seems that on a bleak winter's evening two children were crying bitterly for their mother when the fearsome matron came upon them. She showed not the slightest concern and heartlessly locked the poor infants in a room with neither light nor heat. That night saw a dreadful frost in Derry and a couple of days later the two forgotten youngsters were found frozen to death. There was the usual hue and cry but an enquiry's report made no recommendations. And there the matter should have rested except for the matron's uncharacteristic pangs of conscience. As the days passed she became so guilt-ridden about the incident that she lost control of her senses. Soon she was constantly scouring the rooms and the corridors of the workhouse in search of the children, now of course long dead.

In the end the distraught and deluded matron died, I suppose, of remorse. If she was troublesome before her death it was nothing compared to what was about to happen. One evening not long after her demise her apparition was seen by some of the inmates, walking through the dayroom. Then she began to appear in the sick ward and in the passageways, always searching and seemingly totally demented. As you might guess, the workhouse inmates became completely terrorised by this awful spirit. Some reports say that even the cries of the dead children were heard as she wandered about. Things got so bad that eventually the guardians called in an exorcist in a bid to oust the ghost of the Matron in Blue. Now the story gets really chilling, for when the exorcist challenged the spirit it refused to leave the workhouse. Reports reveal a terrifying scene: in a frenzy the menacing spectre was forced down the corridor towards the door at the top of the thirteen steps but would go no further.

It seemed to be an impasse and that dreadful night of the exorcism looms large in the annals of the Waterside workhouse. Apparently, the only option for the exhausted exorcist was to force the unearthly creature into the nearby dispensary, which had no windows. This way of confining a spirit is believed to be a last resort where exorcisms prove difficult. With the entity at last contained, the dispensary door was locked and completely sealed. Then comes an absolutely bizarre twist in the story: the key to the dispensary door was secretly hidden under the top step at the workhouse front door – the ominous thirteenth step – the idea being, I suppose, that the key was better outside than inside. Thereafter members of staff would not go down the dispensary corridor unaccompanied. Meanwhile, provision had been made for another dispensary elsewhere. I myself have spoken to one nurse who would not go near that corridor under any circumstances. No surprise then that the whole area around the dispensary became laden with foreboding. I was told that there was a sort of heaviness in the air.

And I suppose the Matron in Blue would have stayed there, had it not been for construction work on the newly expanding Waterside Hospital in the 1940s. Unwisely, perhaps, the dispensary door was forced opened during the redevelopment and suddenly the ghost was free to start its wanderings again. The workman involved did not know about the story but described something like a rush of air that made his hair stand on end as he levered the door open. Afterwards came the reports of sightings of the apparition in the wards of the Waterside Hospital.

So is it all a lot of nonsense? I'm afraid not. An incident back in the 1920s indicates just how seriously the residents of the locality took the workhouse ghost. It happened that as road traffic increased, plans were drawn up for the removal of the bend on Glendermott Road, which is just beside the workhouse. However, there was an immediate outcry from the local people when it became known that part of the scheme involved the removal of the thirteen steps that led up to the workhouse door. The feeling not expressed openly was that the key under the thirteenth step would be discovered and the dispensary opened, thereby releasing the dreaded ghoul. Protests became so vigorous that the plans were eventually scrapped and the thirteen steps remain to this day. Even recent major road works on Glendermott Road have left the spot untouched.

Having found no sign of the Matron in Blue in the workhouse on my recent visit, I decided to have another look at the infamous thirteen steps before I left. Indeed there are still thirteen. I counted them carefully and climbed up and down several times, trying to get a sense of times past. I have to say it did feel quite spooky in the winter half-light. Is there a rusty old key underneath that thirteenth step at the top, I wondered. You know, if there is, and even if I didn't see her on this occasion, the Matron in Blue must still be wandering the old Waterside workhouse.

River Foyle Ferries

Steam ferry: from Middle Quay at Harbour Office to Waterside Quay at Northern Counties Railway Station runs every ten minutes – cost 1 penny.

Garrison Ferry (McKeever's): from Middle Quay to Ebrington Barracks; boats always available – cost 1 penny.

Newspaper advertisement

FOOTSTEPS

Someone or Something Came into the Room....

I've not the slightest doubt that the Spencer Road house was haunted and, odd to relate, the name given to the ghost was 'Footsteps'. This tale came to me from people who had lived there and some of their stories were chilling, to say the least. The family in question had just returned to Derry from England in the early 1900s: father, mother, and several children. They were happy to get back home, for the Great War was looming. Naturally they needed somewhere to stay. However, the father's heart fell when he was offered a certain house on Spencer Road in the Waterside, as strange stories were already circulating about this particular dwelling.

To get the sense of this weird affair you have to go back many decades to the days when Spencer Road was not long in existence. The road was constructed to allow the new Carlisle Bridge to connect Derry to the Waterside. At the beginning of the 1900s it was a much quieter street than it is today. In fact it was a lonely thoroughfare, especially at night. At first the parents in our story said they would not take the house but as there was nowhere else they reluctantly moved in. The dwelling was large, dark and quite gloomy inside. There was a ground floor, a first floor and an attic storey with four bedrooms. Half-way up there was a back return with a bathroom and, as you might imagine, there were several staircases.

One of the children recalled many years later how she had scrambled up to the top of the house to explore on that first day. There, in one of the attic rooms, she discovered a cast-iron bedstead. Strangely, it sat right in the centre of the room. She said you could walk right round it and that there was something odd about the bed. For want of a better word, it had an uncomfortable feeling, a sense of a presence. This particular bed was the scene of mighty sinister happenings right from the beginning. That very first night it was made up for two of the younger children and they were duly tucked in by their parents. An hour later noises were heard coming from the room and the mother rushed up, thinking the children were larking about. They were not but they maintained that earlier the door had opened on its own and that the bed had moved by itself.

A worse and more frightening disturbance was yet to come. In the middle of the night the coverings and the children were violently swept off the bed on to the floor. As it happened there seemed to be a great rush of wind through the house, even though it was calm outside. All the windows in the dwelling rattled and woke everyone up. As you might guess the youngsters spent the rest of the night in their parents' bed in the lower storey.

Noises continued to come from the attic room and the family never used it again during all the years they remained in the house – in fact they put a padlock on it. And remain they did for decades, as it seems they got used to whatever presence was there. Perhaps it would be better to say that it, what ever it was, had got used to them. It the early days it seemed as if the ghost was testing them out. One of the most common phenomena was the sound of footsteps on the stairs. These footsteps were heard at all hours of the day and the night and on all the stairways. Sometimes the steps would be heavy and menacing and at other times they were light and playful, almost impish. Sometimes, too, the spooky presence would linger menacingly on a creaky step, then go down a few more steps and come back up. For this reason the family gave the ghost the name 'Footsteps'.

Most times Footsteps would not come down the full stairway to the kitchen – yet occasionally he (for some reason it was thought to be a man) would come right down and hover outside the door as if to say, 'Tonight I am going to reveal myself.' One of the family told me that they were all in the kitchen one evening when Footsteps descended as usual and the handle of the door turned as if it was about to open. Naturally, it made their blood run cold and there was a huge sigh of relief when the steps retreated up again. Another time one of the girls was waiting for her mother to come out of the bathroom on the back return when the steps came up the stairs right past her and on up to the attic.

It also appears the father had a very frightening experience on an occasion when most of the family was away on holidays. An older daughter stayed behind to make his meals. One evening she bade him goodnight as usual about 11pm and the following morning brought a cup of tea to his bedroom. He was not there and after a search she found him asleep, curled up in a blanket in the sitting room. He would not say what took him there and later that day he put a padlock on his bedroom, declaring it out of bounds for everyone from then on. It was not until many years later that he disclosed what had happened. Someone or something came into the room during the night and stood over his bed. Almost paralysed with fear, he managed to force out a prayer and watched as the apparition backed its way out of the room and straight through the closed door. Spookily enough this meant that two rooms in the house were now padlocked.

What did Footsteps look like? We have some idea from what a couple of the very young children described several years on. They slept in a large cot and told me that a kind gentleman often came to say goodnight to them. This was something that their parents were unaware of. The man was small, with a round friendly smiling face and thick old-fashioned sideburns. He would simply appear from nowhere, wearing a green jacket and a light-coloured waistcoat with a silver watch chain, which he would dangle over the edge of the cot in a strange way.

The family eventually moved from Spencer Road but I had the opportunity to have a quick look at the house before they left. I found it extremely dark and brooding. The attic in particular had a very spooky feeling about it. The room that had previously been locked was now open and, remarkably, the iron bedstead was still there. I climbed the stairs a few times and was able to see where Footsteps had come and gone on his nightly wanderings – and I did find the creaky step half-way down where he had hovered so menacingly. More sinister were the bars across the inside of some of the upper windows. I was told these were not to keep thieves from breaking in but to stop people jumping out in fear during the night. These bars had been there before the family in our story came to the house and were fixed on high windows, well away from potential burglars.

So I started to research what had been happening in the dwelling before they came to live in it. You may remember that the father did not want to take this particular place. What I discovered was enough to make me understand his concerns. There were regular complaints of noise by the neighbours even when the house was empty; accounts of terrorised folk rushing into the street in panic in the middle of the night; lights coming off and on by themselves and other happenings better left untold.

The house is still there on Spencer Road and, I think, from whisperings I have heard recently, so is Footsteps.

THE DEVIL AT STUMPIE'S BRAE

Have ye heird nae talk of Stumpie's Brae,
Down by the Foyle where a cottage lay?
Come closer to me one and aw
'Till a tell ye how the de'il did call.

Fancy an encounter with the devil? In times past you might just have had your chance at Stumpie's Brae, which is on the road from Derry to Lifford in County Donegal. The spot is not far from the village of St Johnston and is one of those places that you get a strange feeling about straight away – an oppressive heaviness that is certainly not helped by the shadowy woods and bleak hillsides nearby. As for the tale itself – a legend in these parts – it occurs to me that there's a spiteful wickedness about it. The original story in the form of a poem was unearthed by none other than the famous hymn-writer Cecil Frances Alexander, who knew the locality intimately. I am quite sure she would have visited Stumpie's Brae to see the scene of the spooky goings on for herself and hear the poem recited in the strong local dialect.

So, with the help of C.F. Alexander's poem, adapted in modern idiom, come with me now back to an autumn in the early years of the 1800s as we watch this chilling yarn unfold. Firstly, picture a tiny cottage within sight of the River Foyle. It is a night when a full-blown storm whips the river into a fury and the sky is creased by jagged bolts of lightening, with great peals of thunder echoing into the distant hills. Inside a little dwelling a farmer and his wife sit by the dying embers of their turf fire as the wind outside wails like a banshee. There is not much in the way of conversation between the miserable pair, for their bleak existence usually fosters nothing but ill-humour. Mind you, affairs do brighten on those odd times they get the opportunity to steal from a passer-by. No chance of that, one would have thought, on such an awful night as this – or was there?

Just after midnight a brattle of thunder that seemed to rip the sky apart was followed by a loud, menacing thump upon the cottage door. It marked the beginning of a frightful episode of wickedness and terror:

> *Just as the wind did roar and roar*
> *A knock like death came upon the door*
> *Flung open wide it did reveal*
> *A pedlar man…and the thunder pealed!*
> *'Can ye give me a bed?' says he with a leer.*
> *'I can pay ye well of that no fear.*
> *Aye…have no doubt for my bed I'll pay*
> *For heaps of gold I made this day…'*

At the mention of gold the farmer and his wife smiled slyly at one another; fate had brought them a prize picking right out of the storm. Suddenly their welcome was a friendly one.

'Take yon corner under the stairs,' the farmer motioned to the pedlar. There was a strangeness about their visitor. He was a tall lean man, sharp-featured, with deep-sunk beady eyes, yellow, leathery skin, and a sack over his shoulder. He said he had been to Derry market and had set out on his journey along the river before the bad weather had set in. But was that true? Despite the storm there was not a drop of rain on their visitor's tunic, nor, for that matter, was there a spot of mud on his shiny black boots. It was odd to say, the least of it. Where on earth had he come from?

Once in the corner the pedlar unpacked the sack and proceeded to count his day's takings, his every move watched by the farmer and his wife. They were bewitched by the glint of gold, their hungry eyes growing ever wider as the pedlar teasingly counted sovereign after sovereign into his purse – twenty in all. And in that instant, seized by their greed, the wicked pair decided that the pedlar's gold should be theirs:

> *There came a gleam in the farmer's eye*
> *And a voice in his head said… 'Pedlar die!'*
> *So in the dark when their visitor slept*
> *Up alongside him the pair of them crept;*
> *Then a pick they sank in the pedlar's head*
> *And they banged it in 'till he was dead.*

Swiftly the murderous couple set about searching the pedlar's pack until they came upon the purse with the gold coins:

> *'Look at his gold!' they cried with delight*
> *And they danced with joy on that evil night.*

However, in the midst of their jubilation it suddenly struck them that they had a dead body on their hands. What would they do with it? Then the farmer's crafty wife had an idea: 'Put him into his own sack and dump him in the bog,' said she coldly. She hurriedly flung the contents of the sack upon the floor – toys, trinkets, bric-a-brac, flying everywhere. But as fate would have it, they could not get the pedlar's corpse completely into the empty sack. However much they tried his long legs kept dangling out over the top – it was almost as if those legs had a life of their own. What next for the evil pair? The wife thought for a while and then proposed something just about as wicked as any human being could conjure up. 'Cut him off at the knees!' snapped she cruelly. 'Then we'll drag him up the brae in the sack and dig a good hole for him.' And this they did, burying the pedlar, without the slightest remorse, in the cold damp earth of the bog beside the brae.

Now comes something deeply chilling. As the farmer and

his wife were making their way back down the brae to the cottage the corpse in the pack sat bolt upright. Then, breaking through the clay it uttered a fearsome curse that echoed across the bog and far beyond:

> 'You think ye laid me snug in clay
> But I shall rise in night or day
> And I'll haunt ye far and I'll haunt ye near –
> Father and son with terror and fear
> Across the seas and every nation
> Right down to the nineteenth generation!'

Frightening to relate, next evening, as the farmer and his wife drooled over their ill-gotten gold, what can only be described as a bloodcurdling haunting began. Firstly, their dog yelped and cowered away under the table. Then came a strange dragging noise – a slithery sound, followed by a hollow knock on the cottage door, which burst open to reveal none other than the dead pedlar, or what was left of him. His head was spattered with blood and worst of all he moved upon his stumps, the bare bones of his knees, where his legs had been hacked off. And round and round the cottage all night long the spectre chased the wicked pair until first light, by which time the wife's hair had turned white and the farmer was stooped and visibly aged. Night after night it continued, with the ghost, now well-named 'Stumpie', each time more menacing and always announced by the noise of his terrifying slither.

> There came each night a terrible slither,
> A stumpie sound going hither and thither.

In the end the farmer and his wife fled to America, taking a McCorkell ship from Derry Quay, in the hope that the New World would free them from Stumpie's ghastly curse. But it was not to be; as he had said:

'And I'll haunt ye far and I'll haunt ye near
Father and son with terror and fear.'

Stumpie was even heard slithering along the deck of the ship on the voyage out from Derry and continued to blight the life of the farmer and his wife in America until their dying day. Worse still, Stumpie's dreadful prophesy about haunting the family down to the nineteenth generation is still being fulfilled. Definitions of a generation differ but if we take twenty-five years as an average, Stumpie's nineteenth generation curse has several hundred years to run. The family, who still live in America, are aware of it but their names must not be mentioned for reasons of sensitivity. These days, although they do not see the spectre of Stumpie, they still feel his presence through the ghastly sound of his slither, despite all attempts to exorcise the ghost.

And should you be brave enough to wander down by Stumpie's Brae near the River Foyle as the light goes of an evening, do keep in mind the menacing words of Cecil Frances Alexander about that little cottage:

Ye'll ken it well, through the few fir trees
An if ye meet ane there, as daylight flees
Stumping about on the banes o' his knees,
It'll just be oul Stumpie himself' tae please!

BOOM HALL

Tales of a Ghost and a Mysterious Guest

Boom Hall is a sad ruin these days. It sits in the trees on the Derry side of the Foyle Bridge and as you wander about this lonely place you cannot but feel a hint of mystery in the air. This is no surprise, really, for there were two weird happenings here that have not been explained to this day. The name comes from the floating boom placed across the river Foyle at this spot during the siege in 1689 but the house was not built until ninety years later. In its day it was an elegant Georgian residence but now only the ivy-clad walls and four rather forlorn chimney stacks remain.

Yet Boom Hall saw more than a hundred and fifty years of vibrant life, having been occupied by the Alexanders until 1840; then by families much associated with Derry's great sailing days, the Bairds, the Corscaddens and the Cookes. The strange atmosphere that surrounds Boom Hall today invites claims of ghostly sightings and indeed there have been many of these, especially in the wooded grounds, which slope gently towards the Foyle. Whatever about such reports, it is from the days of the Alexander family that we find really mysterious stories about the house.

In the early years of the nineteenth century the Alexanders established themselves as merchants in Derry and Limavady, where the original Alexander Bank was in time to become part of the Bank of Ireland. Some of the family made fortunes overseas and others still became renowned for their achievements – among them Field Marshall Alexander of

Second World War fame and the brilliant William Alexander, formerly the Protestant Bishop of Derry (1867-1896) and later Primate of Ireland (1896-1911). It was this same William Alexander, the Derry bishop and husband of Cecil Frances, the well-known hymnist, who handed down our strange stories. His father Robert was born at Boom Hall and William frequently visited the old house along the Foyle. In later years William kept his personal memories of the family in what he called his 'tin box'. This became a treasure-chest of anecdotes about the Alexanders but it wasn't until the contents were examined after his death in 1911 that two astonishing stories came to light.

The first of these told of the apparition of a young boy, Waller Alexander. Waller was born in the early 1800s and was a much-loved child in the household. Ever energetic, he could always be found playing in front of Boom Hall. Then as a treat, to mark his eighth birthday, Waller was taken to visit his grandparents at Drogheda. It was summer time and word came back to Boom Hall that he was enjoying himself immensely and was the centre of attention as usual. Now comes the chilling part of the tale. Early one morning some weeks later Waller's grandmother looked out a landing window at Boom Hall and was surprised to see Waller playing in front of the house as he usually did. You can imagine the old lady's delight when the popular young lad smiled up at her. Later that day she met the boy's mother and asked, 'How on earth did Waller get back home?'

'Goodness, surely you know that Waller's still away on holiday!' came the startled reply.

Old Mrs Alexander felt that something wasn't right but decided to say nothing more. Two days later there came news that horridly confirmed her sense of unease. Inexplicably, young Waller had suddenly died at his grandparents' home in Drogheda and his death had occurred at the same instant old Mrs Alexander had seen him in front of the house in Derry. The appearance of the wraith of a person is taken in Irish folklore to portend death. Clearly what appeared at Boom Hall was Waller Alexander's wraith and the Alexander family firmly believed this story.

The second tale from the 'tin box' concerned the sudden appearance of a young woman in the grounds of Boom Hall, not long after the appearance of Waller's 'fetch'. She was found in a distressed state near the river's edge not far from the house. There were some remarkable things about this young woman. Firstly, she motioned that she could not speak. Secondly, she was magnificently dressed and had a beautiful appearance; she was clearly a high-born lady. As you might guess, the Alexanders were puzzled by the arrival of this mysterious visitor – out of nowhere, as it seemed. But being a compassionate family they decided without a moment's hesitation to give her shelter until more information was forthcoming.

Months went by without any explanation, so eventually the unfortunate woman went below stairs to work in the Boom Hall kitchen. She never spoke and in her spare time occupied herself with needlework, something at which she excelled. Her constant companion was young Robert Alexander, Waller's brother. It seems that Robert was the only one who could bring a smile to the stranger's face, for she was frequently lost in a flood of tears. Indeed some said she was pining away.

Then came an amazing turn of events. One day, out of the blue, during some sort of disturbance in the kitchen, the mysterious woman suddenly started babbling in a tongue unknown to anyone – and this included the Alexanders, who had arrived to see what was going on. Later, some people suggested that the language might be Portuguese and this became all the more intriguing when it was revealed that a ship from Portugal had been in Derry port some time back. Meanwhile, it was evident that the woman was becoming more and more ill. Her only consolation was young Robert Alexander and as a reward for keeping her company she made him a most magnificent quilt. The design was said to be breathtaking and the quilt was handed down through many generations of the Alexanders. Not long after the quilt was completed the woman died of what must be described as a broken heart. There was much debate about her fate and in the end the Alexanders concluded that she might have been rejected in love. One solution suggested was that she had been on board a ship and after some sort of quarrel was put ashore on the banks of the Foyle near the Boom Hall residence.

With the passage of time many families came and went from Boom Hall until the Second World War when the Navy commandeered it. Afterwards the McDevitt family purchased the house and they were to be the last residents of this once impressive building, which was gutted by fire in the early 1970s.

AFTERWORD: BOOM HALL AND ITS VISITORS

As you might expect with so many families having occupied Boom Hall since 1779 the old house saw many comings and goings. It became one of Derry's meeting places for the merchant class fraternity, many of whom had intermarried over the generations. So there were often great garden parties – the men in formal attire, the women in magnificent dresses. One famous visitor in the summer of 1849 was Thomas Babington (Lord) Macaulay, the acclaimed historian, although a man not without his critics. Macaulay, said to be one of the finest writers in the English language, was entranced by Derry. He recalls riding by carriage to Boom Hall and meeting the Baird family, that had moved in after the Alexanders. Mrs Baird took him through the grounds to the edge of the river Foyle so that he could inspect the site of the Siege boom, something which later figured in Macaulay's writings.

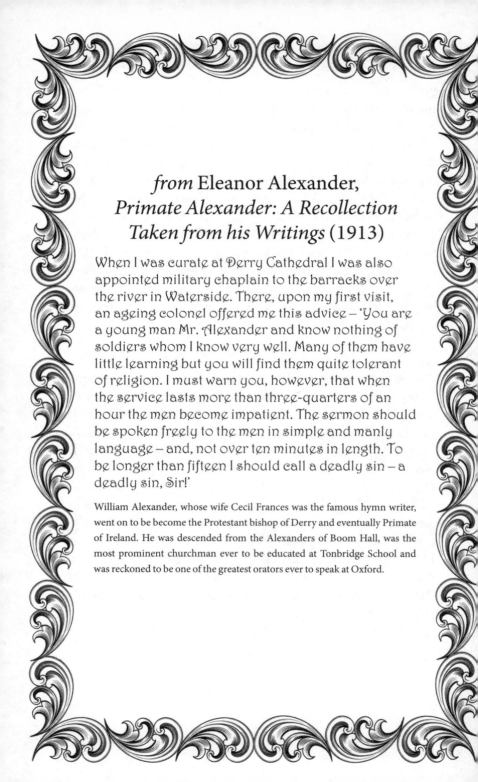

from Eleanor Alexander, *Primate Alexander: A Recollection Taken from his Writings* (1913)

When I was curate at Derry Cathedral I was also appointed military chaplain to the barracks over the river in Waterside. There, upon my first visit, an ageing colonel offered me this advice – 'You are a young man Mr. Alexander and know nothing of soldiers whom I know very well. Many of them have little learning but you will find them quite tolerant of religion. I must warn you, however, that when the service lasts more than three-quarters of an hour the men become impatient. The sermon should be spoken freely to the men in simple and manly language – and, not over ten minutes in length. To be longer than fifteen I should call a deadly sin – a deadly sin, Sir!'

William Alexander, whose wife Cecil Frances was the famous hymn writer, went on to be become the Protestant bishop of Derry and eventually Primate of Ireland. He was descended from the Alexanders of Boom Hall, was the most prominent churchman ever to be educated at Tonbridge School and was reckoned to be one of the greatest orators ever to speak at Oxford.

Bibliography

Alexander, E. (ed). *Primate Alexander Archbishop of Armagh, A Memoir.* London, 1913.

Alexander, C.F.A. 'The Graveyard in the Hills' ('Stumpie's Brae').

Cooke, Sholto. *The Maiden City and the Western Ocean.* Dublin: Morris, *c.* 1950.

Beechey, F.W. *Voyage of Discovery towards the North Pole.* London: Bentley, 1843.

Bryson, J.G. *The Streets of Derry.* Derry: Guildhall Press, 2001.

Colby, T. *Ordnance Survey (Memoir) of Londonderry.* Dublin, 1837.

Coyle, Kathleen. *Magical Realm.* Wolfhound Press: Dublin, 1997 (first published 1943).

Currie, J.R.L. *The Northern Counties Railway.* Newton Abbot: David and Charles, 1973.

Day, A. and P. McWilliams (eds.). *Ordnance Survey Memoirs of Ireland.* Belfast and Dublin, 1990-8.

Gallagher, C. *Acorns and Oak Leaves (A Derry Childhood).* Belfast: Dubh Regles Books, 1973.

Frankcom, G. *et al. The Irish Giant.* London: Duckworth, 1973.

Gilfillan, A. *Diary of a Voyage to the North Pole.* 1818.

Hughes, Sam. *City on the Foyle.* Derry, 1984.

Keay, J. *The Great Arc.* London: Harper Collins, 2000.

Lewis, S. *Topographical Dictionary of Ireland* (1837). Belfast, 2004.

McCann, W. *H.B. Phillips: Impresario.* Belfast: Belfast Society and Ulster Historical Foundation, 2001.

McFadden, V. *Island City.* Derry, 1982.

Milligan, C.D. *History of the Siege of Londonderry, 1689.* Belfast: Carter Publications, 1951.

Mitchell, G.S. *Three Cheers for the Derrys!* Derry: Yes Publications, 1991.

O'Donovan, J. *Letters from County Londonderry (1834).* County Derry: Ballinascreen Historical Society, 1992.

Ogilby, J.D. *The Early Years of a Naturalist* (1853-73). Queensland, Australia, 1925.

Pigott Directory of Ireland (1824).

Prehen (Knox Archive). *Life of John McNaghten.* London, 1762.

Simpson, R. *The Annals of Derry (1847).* Limavady, County Derry: North-West Books, 1987.

Thackeray, W.M. *The Irish Sketch Book 1842.* Dublin: Nonsuch, 2005.

NEWSPAPERS AND PERIODICALS

Foyle and Londonderry College past magazines

The *Derry Journal*; The *Londonderry Sentinel*; The *Londonderry Standard* (1800-1900).